Is It Unpatriotic to Criticize One's Country?

Other books in the At Issue series:

Is It Unpatriotic to Criticize One's Country?

Mary E. Williams, *Book Editor*

Bruce Glassman, *Vice President*
Bonnie Szumski, *Publisher*
Helen Cothran, *Managing Editor*

GREENHAVEN PRESS
An imprint of Thomson Gale, a part of The Thomson Corporation

Detroit • New York • San Francisco • San Diego • New Haven, Conn.
Waterville, Maine • London • Munich

© 2005 Thomson Gale, a part of The Thomson Corporation.

For more information, contact
Greenhaven Press
27500 Drake Rd.
Farmington Hills, MI 48331-3535
Or you can visit our Internet site at http://www.gale.com

LIBRARY OF CONGRESS CATALOGING-IN-PUBLICATION DATA

Is it unpatriotic to criticize one's country? / Mary E. Williams, book editor.
     p. cm. — (At issue)
Includes bibliographical references and index.
ISBN 0-7377-2396-3 (lib. : alk. paper) — ISBN 0-7377-2397-1 (pbk. : alk. paper)
     1. Patriotism—United States. 2. Dissenters—United States. 3. War on Terrorism, 2001– . 4. Christianity and politics—United States. I. Williams, Mary E., 1960– . II. At issue (San Diego, Calif.)
JK1759.I85 2005
323.6'5'0973—dc22   2004059694

Printed in the United States of America

Contents

Introduction

"It looks like a kind of second flowering of spring in early autumn, the way the [American] flags have sprouted everywhere," wrote journalist Rich Heffern one month after the terrorist attacks of September 11, 2001. "Out of the ashes in New York, Washington and Pennsylvania rose a common civic-mindedness completely unprecedented in the lives of many of us," Heffern mused. Indeed, Americans did experience a revival of patriotism in the wake of the most devastating act of terrorism that had ever occurred in their native land. To revere those who had been killed, to honor firefighters, police, and rescue workers, and to express a sense of national unity, citizens displayed American flags at their homes, on their vehicles, and on their clothing. And in the ensuing months, as the Bush administration launched a war on terror that included military campaigns in Afghanistan and Iraq and new national security measures, most citizens believed that it was important to maintain a united front while the nation remained under the threat of attack. Bumper stickers and T-shirts proclaimed "United We Stand" and "God Bless America." American troops who were deployed to Afghanistan and Iraq were hailed as selfless defenders of freedom—and as exemplars of great patriotism for their readiness to sacrifice their lives for American ideals and interests.

But for many, there was a dark side to this patriotic fervor. In the fall of 2001, for example, angry Americans surrounded a Chicago-area mosque, waving flags and shouting "USA! USA!" before being turned back by police. Since the terrorist attacks had been instigated by Osama bin Laden, a radical Islamic fundamentalist, the marchers had viewed all Muslims as suspect. That same fall, California congressional representative Barbara Lee voted against U.S. military retaliation in Afghanistan and received death threats as a result. In addition, Aaron McGruder's cartoon *The Boondocks* was pulled from newspapers around the country for stating that the CIA had helped train terrorists like bin Laden, and Bill Maher's nightly talk show *Politically Incorrect* was taken off the air after Maher challenged George W. Bush's description of the 2001 terrorists as "cowardly." For the first two years after the terrorist attacks, those who openly questioned the U.S. response to the attacks or who suggested that America bore some responsibility for inducing terrorism were often accused of disloyalty, even treason.

In the year 2003 the U.S.-led war in Iraq became the focus of heated debates concerning patriotism and loyalty to country. Initially, most Americans supported the war because the Bush administration claimed that Iraqi dictator Saddam Hussein had weapons of mass destruction and was likely preparing to attack the United States. Hussein was also said to have had a connection with al Qaeda, the group responsible for the 2001 terrorist attacks. After several months passed, however, when no weapons of mass destruction had been found and the connection between Hussein and al Qaeda remained unverified, a growing number of U.S. citizens began to question the legitimacy and the morality of the war.

Interestingly, both prowar and antiwar Americans generally see themselves as patriotic. In the opinion of prowar conservative commentator David Horowitz, for example, patriotism means that in a time of war "you postpone criticism" and "defend your country." In response to antiwar activists, who argue that their criticism of the war is rooted in their deep love of the American ideals of justice and integrity, Horowitz asks, "What is the meaning of patriotism if you don't defend your country?" After all, "Patriotism means that you have to have a fundamental identity and loyalty to America. It means defending the real country, the actual existing country," and not a lofty ideal. But antiwar *Progressive Review* editor Sam Smith maintains that confronting questionable American policies is the highest—though perhaps the more difficult—form of patriotism:

> We justly pledge allegiance to the republic for which America stands, but we do not have to pledge allegiance to . . . the failed policies for which America is now suffering. There are few finer, albeit painful, expressions of loyalty than to tell a friend, a spouse, a child, or a parent that what they are doing may be dangerous or wrong. If our country is about to run into the street without looking, there is absolutely nothing disloyal about crying, "Stop!"

But many wonder whether dissent in itself is a form of patriotism. In the opinion of syndicated columnist David Limbaugh, it is not. While he grants that the *right* to dissent is part of what makes America great, the *act* of dissenting is not necessarily patriotic. "You may dissent to your heart's content," writes Limbaugh, "but the substance of your statements will not be exempted from scrutiny merely because you are exercising rights we consider sacred in America." If the dissent expresses contempt for America, or upholds a kind of global "one worldism" over American sovereignty, it is not an act of patriotism, Limbaugh maintains. Law and ethics professor Martha Nussbaum contends, on the other hand, that patriotic feelings for one's country can too easily degenerate into feelings of superiority and a desire to humiliate or defeat other nations. While a love of one's country is natural, Americans should find ways to empathize with people beyond their borders. Dissent and debate, she argues, can help transform the sympathy that Americans feel for their own people into a broader concern for human vulnerabilities in other nations: "At this time of national crisis we can renew our commitment to the equal worth of humanity, demanding media and schools that nourish and expand our imaginations by presenting non-American lives as deep, rich and compassion-worthy."

Such a divergence of opinion concerning patriotism is not unusual in the United States, particularly during national crises and controversial wars. As the comments of thinkers like Horowitz, Smith, Limbaugh, and Nussbaum suggest, the very definition of patriotism is becoming more complex as citizens reexamine their allegiances and loyalties in a modern multicultural world.

1

Criticizing One's Country Can Be Patriotic

Al Martinez

Al Martinez is a columnist for the Los Angeles Times.

The United States is a great nation because it allows its people the right to openly disagree with the majority of the population. Patriotism does not require citizens to blindly follow misguided leaders or to support wars based on lies and immoral reasoning. Americans have the right to protest government policies that violate their consciences, to vote or to not vote, and to doubt what they hear and read in the media. One can question the powerful, challenge the status quo, and hold unpopular opinions while remaining deeply committed to America.

I was listening to a superpatriot the other day saying what a great country we have and how criticism of its motives weakens the solid front we should be offering the world in these difficult times.

He was a Bush apologist who was using patriotism to cover up the fact that we have gotten ourselves into one fine mess in Iraq, but that's neither here nor there. What struck me was the solid-front business he was promulgating.

I tolerated his rant as politely as I could, but when I couldn't take it any longer I said, "You know what's truly great about this country? You don't have to be part of a solid front if you don't want to."

I ended my discussion with the guy on that note, and as I thought about it later, I realized how much grandeur there was in negativity when one considers freedom. Inherent in its rights, you see, is the right not to.

The concept is particularly significant on this Independence Day weekend, when we celebrate the precepts that have made us different from much of the world.

The Right to Disagree

We have the right not to participate in that solid front if it violates our conscience. We can stand aside, ignore it or protest in a way of our choosing. If our choice involves mass demonstrations, that's a right too, the right not to assemble peaceably but to take part in displays of civil disobedience to make a point.

We have a choice to disobey police orders and not to yield to the truncheons and tear gas of the blue army, and not to beg for lenience if protest puts us behind bars.

We have the right not to remain silent when giving voice to the innocence and the passion of our causes, even when speaking out brands us as something less than patriotic.

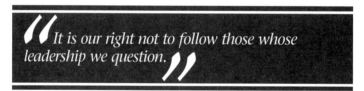

It is our right not to follow those whose leadership we question.

These fundamental freedoms to choose, to make up our own minds, overlap with one of America's most fundamental rights: the right to vote, to elect our own leaders, to define our own future. That also includes the right not to vote if we don't want to, and most of us don't. We can take our chances with choices made by that small portion of the population that does go to the polls. And even then, it's our right not to like what we get and to moan about our fate, even though we did nothing to prevent it.

The Liberty That Options Imply

It's our right not to believe what we hear or what we read, because doubt is an integral part of freedom. It is similarly our right not to idolize leadership but to recognize that human weaknesses exist even among those who make stupendous decisions. It is our right not to follow those whose leadership we question.

It is our right not to believe in God and to mock those who do, without fear of incarceration, torture or death. We can be atheists if we desire, and we can scorn those who use religion to debase humanity, who trumpet the Lord to justify their excesses.

It is our right to defy the jingoism that accompanies a drive to war, and our right to believe that those who die in war are more victim than hero. It is our right to shake our heads when we hear the parents of a dead soldier say they were proud that he died that way, instead of saying that he didn't have to die that way at all, torn by shrapnel, facedown in a ditch, bleeding into the sand.

We have the right in this land of rights not to accept the status quo but to challenge the stars in the name of destiny, to dare and sometimes to lose. We have the right to establish by losing that a truly free country allows for its failures and the learning that accompanies the grief when stars fall from the sky.

It is our right, Americans, to turn our backs on the freedoms that allow us to turn our backs. We can sit as the flag passes and, by our gesture, defy those around us who stand, hands over their hearts, solid citizens as tall and straight as boards, honoring the colors that fill the sky. And we can remain silent when the national anthem is sung, without tears in our eyes or a lump in our throats.

We can understand, as I always try to understand, the strengths encompassed by protest, by individuality, by the willingness to risk all for an idea whose time has come. I can't think of a better way to honor our country than by honoring the concept of choice and the liberty that options imply.

This is the power of my belief in America, and the soul of my commitment to it. And if there are tears in my heart and a shiver up my spine as I sit alone and sing of my country in a different way, it is only because I know I can. It's my right.

2
Criticizing One's Country Is Not Patriotic

David Limbaugh

David Limbaugh is a nationally syndicated columnist.

The right to political dissent is a freedom that Americans should be proud of. However, the act of dissenting should not be equated with patriotism. Dissent cannot be patriotic if the denigration of American leaders and U.S. policy constitutes the substance of the dissent. Those who openly express contempt for America—such as the extreme leftists who protested the U.S.-led war against Saddam Hussein's regime in Iraq—are not exhibiting patriotism. True patriotism requires a love of America and a reverence for America's uniqueness and sovereignty.

Many extreme leftists have a funny idea about patriotism. The more they show their disgust with America—especially on foreign soil—the better patriots they believe they are.

First we had David "Baghdad" Bonior and Congressman Jim McDermott parading around the streets of [Baghdad, Iraq] decrying President [George W.] Bush and the United States and saying Iraq had no weapons of mass destruction. McDermott suggested that Bush would knowingly mislead the American people in furtherance of his war aims against Iraq, and was planning to attack Iraq as part of a plot to crown himself "Emperor of America." While it's probably fair to say this regrettable delegation doesn't represent the Democratic Party, it's noteworthy that when pressed, few, if any Democrats condemned these men for their contemptible behavior.

David Limbaugh, "Dissent Does Not Equal Patriotism," *Conservative Chronicle*, vol. 18, March 14, 2003, p. 7. Copyright © 2003 by Creators Syndicate. Reproduced by permission of the author.

Then the erudite actor Sean Penn made a complete moron of himself stumping for [Iraqi leader Saddam Hussein] in Iraq before realizing he'd been duped, and actor Danny Glover, while in Brazil, called President Bush, instead of Sean Penn, a moron. There have been plenty of others, but more recently the Dixie Chicks in a live performance in London said they were sorry President Bush was from Texas.

Super Patriots?

As passionately as these people castigate President Bush and American policy, they are equally passionate about their patriotism. You don't dare question their patriotism. Indeed they are proving themselves to be super patriots through the very act of dissenting. Without them, we are led to believe, the First Amendment would just dry up and blow away. (Personally, I'll be more convinced of their indiscriminate passion for free expression when I see them lobbying against college speech codes and the like.)

Let's get something straight. As much as they practice the art, the far left has a limited comprehension of the role of dissent, the concept of patriotism and their ostensible interrelationship.

Liberals confuse the *right* to dissent with the *act* of dissenting. My liberal friend Alan Colmes recently said, "I think protesting is actually very pro-American. It's what a democracy really is."

No, Alan, protesting against America is not "very pro-American." Being pro-America is pro-American. Defending one's *right* to protest is celebrating America's freedoms. But the act of dissing America while exercising those freedoms is not pro-American.

It is not the act of dissenting that makes this country great. There is nothing noble in trashing America and her leaders on foreign soil, especially as we prepare for war against a foreign country.[1] It is disgraceful. Antiwar protestors are not exhibiting their patriotism when they dissent; they are exercising their freedoms—and there's a big difference.

The right to dissent—included in the First Amendment—is part of what makes America great (but far from the only thing).

---

1. This refers to the U.S.-led war against Saddam Hussein's regime in Iraq. The war began in March 2003.

That right carries with it a duty of responsibility and a measure of accountability, such as incurring the scorn of the many who do love this country. You may dissent to your heart's content, but the substance of your statements will not be exempted from scrutiny merely because you are exercising rights we consider sacred in America. You are not fooling many people by wrapping yourself in the flag of dissent, trying to pretend that it, too, is red, white and blue.

Loving America

Patriotism is not about worshipping dissent. It is about love of country. Since when are expressions of contempt considered outpourings of love? It is about appreciating America's uniqueness, including her unparalleled freedoms, not about casually dismissing America's sovereignty in favor of one worldism or love poems about "our common humanity."

Patriotism is not "talking across national boundaries" as part of "a global debate about this war," as the *Nation*'s Bruce Shapiro lamely characterized Hollywood's antiwar drumbeat. Nor is it "pledg(ing) to make common cause with the people of the world to bring about justice, freedom and peace," as Hollywood leftists and others did in their "Not in Our Name" diatribe [against the Iraq War].

> *Protesting against America is not 'very pro-American.' Being pro-America is pro-American.*

It is not patriotic for antiwar protestors to burn and rip up flags, flowers and patriotic signs that residents had erected on a fence along Whittier Boulevard in California to commemorate those lost when this nation was attacked on September 11, 2001. And it's not patriotic for antiwar types to try to censor the unmistakably patriotic song of country star Darryl Worley about 9/11, "Have You Forgotten?"

By no means are all those opposed to war against Iraq being unreasonable. But those extreme leftist antiwar protestors are different. They have every right to belittle this nation as it prepares for war, but they shouldn't expect to be exalted for it.

3

Patriotism Should Be Enshrined in America

Patrick H. Brady

Retired U.S. Army major general Patrick H. Brady is a Medal of Honor recipient who served two tours during the Vietnam War. He is chair of the Citizens Flag Alliance.

A patriot loves, upholds, and willingly makes sacrifices to defend his or her country. As such, patriotism is vital to a nation's survival. While debate is necessary, American patriots should never allow dissent to undermine the law of the land or the wisdom of common people. The liberal elite of educators, lawyers, journalists, and celebrities are not patriots because their ideals and causes do not reflect traditional American values, morality, or justice. Some of the elite are especially dangerous because they condemn the war on terrorism, tolerate evil ideas, and promote the passage of immoral laws. They should be denounced as domestic enemies. In the meantime children must be instilled with a love of their country and a willingness to make sacrifices to protect America's freedoms.

On Sept. 11, 2001, America was stunned by a terrorist attack. The surprising outpouring of patriotism that followed equally stunned us. For some time, a strong majority of Americans felt patriotism was in serious decline. But since Sept. 11, more people are buying and flying flags than at any time in history. It is possible that we have never been more united in support of each other and our troops. The terrorists have put our hands over our hearts again, and this renewed patriotism

Patrick H. Brady, "The Last Refuge of a Free People," *American Legion Magazine*, vol. 154, September 2002, pp. 44, 46, 48. Copyright © 2002 by *American Legion Magazine*. Reproduced by permission.

exhilarates most of us—but not all.

The leftist elite in America are fond of finding good in conduct the majority finds evil or offensive, such as the ACLU's [American Civil Liberties Union's] defense of flag desecration and pedophilic solicitation of our children on the Internet as "free speech." Not surprisingly, these elite also find evil in good—patriotism, for example. Notables from Dr. Samuel Johnson to Albert Einstein have condemned patriotism, and some television networks actually discouraged their work force from wearing patriotic symbols after the Sept. 11 massacre.

> *The terrorists have put our hands over our hearts again, and this renewed patriotism exhilarates most of us—but not all.*

In a recent House debate on whether or not flag burning is constitutionally protected "speech," one member ridiculed the patriotism of those who disagreed with his tirade that burning the symbol of patriotism is patriotic. Another member said it was probably a debate on the definition of patriotism. It is hard to believe we have lawmakers with opposing definitions of patriotism. President [Abraham] Lincoln taught us that a nation divided cannot survive. A nation with different definitions of the Constitution and patriotism is a nation divided. For that reason, it is vital that all Americans understand patriotism, why it is important and why it is controversial. What follows is a look at genuine patriots and why they are vital, counterfeit patriots and why they are dangerous, and why the elite are wrong when they insist that patriotism not be forced.

The Genuine Patriot

A patriot is one who loves, supports and defends one's country. That is not a version of the word; that is the definition. "Support" and "defend" are the operative words; note that the definition does not focus on war. Love is difficult to pin down, best known by its fruits. To understand the love of a patriot, it is important to understand that sacrifice is best defined as love in action. Those who willingly sacrifice, i.e. support and defend, do so out of love. But the love of a patriot is not blind. Just as it is impossible to care for a person and not correct him, one cannot care for America and not seek to correct its errors.

We must guarantee that dissent and debate are robust but never damage or are directed against our Constitution, the foundation of our freedoms. Jefferson said, "I readily suppose my opinion is wrong, when opposed by the majority" and "it is my principle that the will of the majority should always prevail." It is the wisdom of the people, ultimately the majority of an informed active people, that is our protection from tyranny. The elite minority has no right to rule and should never do so.

Country is easily defined as the people, our neighbors, the land and our leaders. One need not love his neighbors, but he may not harm them. That is against the law. One may not love the land, but he may not pollute it. Is protecting our people and our land forcing patriotism? Yes. Is it forcing patriotism to draft citizens to give their lives in war to protect and defend their country? Certainly. Is it forcing patriotism to force our citizens to ration in time of war to support the effort? You bet. We may not love our leaders, but we are obliged to obey their laws.

Is it forcing patriotism to force obedience to the law? What are laws for if not to force the unpatriotic to act patriotic? Patriots, good citizens, don't need laws. Any person who accepts the protection and prosperity of a nation ought to be obedient to the laws of that nation and willing to support and defend it in peace and at war.

> *A patriot is one who loves, supports and defends one's country.*

No one has a right to control what anyone thinks, believes or loves, but we have every right, indeed an obligation, to control how our citizens act. It is insane to say that a free people cannot control conduct, and that it is not patriotic to do so. It should be obvious that demanding—indeed, forcing—patriotism is the bedrock of our freedom. It also should be clear that patriotism is the lifeblood of any nation. No nation can survive if its people refuse to support and defend it. Lukewarm Americans are indifferent to the demands of patriotism and much else, but the uncommon common Americans accept it. The elite do not.

The Booted and Spurred Elite

To understand the elite's distaste for patriotism, it helps to understand them. They have been best defined as those who believe they were born with boots and spurs and the rest of us with saddles on our back. They are obsessed with personal power and sprinkled generously throughout our most influential forums—the classrooms, the courtrooms, the cloakrooms and the newsrooms. They seldom are found in the boardrooms, the factories or the farms, and they are never found in veterans' cemeteries. They have little concern with our posterity but much for their own prosperity. They speak much of peace, not out of interest in peace but for fear they may have to sacrifice for it. The booted and spurred scoff at sacrifice. Sacrifice is for the saddled. Their most prominent characteristic may be physical cowardice. For them, morality is relative. So is patriotism, and toleration of evil is their supreme good.

> 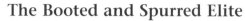 *It should be obvious that demanding—indeed, forcing—patriotism is the bedrock of our freedom.*

They can rationalize evil. Many are the leftover Left of the 1960s, some still enamored with communism. Their heroes are celebrities. They are fond of saying the American flag is just a piece of cloth. Desecrating it is protected "speech," and so is pornography; however, prayer is not, and the Ten Commandments are a danger to the public.

The booted and spurred are represented by college professors who praised the terrorists' attack and blamed America for it; by journalists like Mike Wallace, who said he would refuse to prevent the massacre of American soldiers in order to get a story; and by lawyers, some wearing black robes over their boots and spurs, who attack justice and morality and promote laws that do not reflect our values. Their weary mantra of one man's filth is another man's lyric has become "your terrorist is my freedom fighter."

The uncommon common Americans don't mind the saddle. They accept the fact that they may be rode hard and put away wet. In their ranks are the discarded—the blind, the lame, the insane and those who have been fodder for the forces of freedom. Their sweat lubricates the machinery of America, and their blood nourishes the tree of liberty. The uncommon common Americans fill veterans' cemeteries. They love peace but know there are worse things than war, and they all come with defeat. Their dominant characteristics are courage and humility. They are team players and find happiness in sacrifice. God is their supreme good. They cannot rationalize evil. They despise communism. Their heroes are each other. They love the American flag and say desecrating it is hateful conduct.

They are represented by men like Webster Anderson, a triple amputee from Vietnam, who told a group of youngsters that he only had one arm left, but his country could have it any time it wished. We saw the uncommon common Americans at work in the New York rubble after Sept. 11—the firefighters and police, the equipment operators, the pick-and-axe-and-shovel Americans who bled and poured sweat to save their fellow Americans. The men who raised the American flag in the wreckage of the Twin Towers weren't wearing $1,000 suits or black robes.

The Anti-Patriot and Faux Patriot

Mixed in among the booted and spurred are the anti-patriots and the faux patriots. They are the domestic enemy we all swore to protect and defend our Constitution against. The anti-patriots are easily identified. They claim to hate America for our ideology, but in truth it is because of their evil. The lobby to tolerate evil has given them haven in America; it nurtures this cancer among us. The faux patriots are the most dangerous.

> *The faux patriots thrive in the media, where we hear American journalists separating journalism in America from America [and] where they denounce our war on terrorism.*

These people are contra-constitutionalists engaged in guerilla warfare against our Constitution. They seek to unconstitutionally change the country of our founders to fit their agenda. They profess to love America yet refuse to support or defend it, like a parent claiming to love a child but refusing to care for that child or defend him. The faux patriots bristle at being called unpatriotic; they cower behind their "love" of America. It is their shield from the hardship and danger of service to America. The "love" gambit is vital to them; if flag burners are not patriots, and they are not, how can those who support flag burning be patriots? Like everything else, the "love" of the elite is superior and more sophisticated to that of the saddled Americans.

> *Every law we pass should foster love of country, and every parent, teacher, public figure, role model and hero should be a patriot.*

The faux patriots thrive in the media, where we hear American journalists separating journalism in America from America; where they denounce our war on terrorism, praise the courage of our enemy, and would expose our secrets and endanger our soldiers for a story. When the poet spoke of patriotism as the last refuge of scoundrels, these were the scoundrels he was speaking about.

The booted and spurred promote an America of unlovable people and laws, people and laws which will not nurture patriotism or inspire the sacrifice needed for survival. Many veterans in recent years have said that what America is becoming is not the America they fought for, and they would not fight for it again. The elite are changing our Constitution and our country, making us a less lovable people, and that is why they are dangerous. In another era, many of the booted and spurred would be branded traitors.

Changing Times for Patriotism

In my opinion, earlier generations would have executed Jane Fonda.[1] Can you imagine her frolicking atop a Nazi V2 rocket and then being hailed as one of the century's top 100 female role models? Today I can't see Hanoi Jane celebrating tea with a terrorist in an al-Qaida cave and returning home a heroine. Sept. 11 changed that. On that day we discovered that the pa-

---

1. In 1972 actor Jane Fonda traveled to Hanoi in North Vietnam and protested the Vietnam War.

triotism many feared lost was only dormant, kept alive over the years by the American family and organizations like The American Legion. Sept. 11 marked not only the death rattle for terrorism, but a monumental victory for hard hats over boots and spurs—a victory of those who wear their patriotism on their sleeve over those who will not wear a flag on their lapel.

Now is not the time to bask in this triumph. It is time to consolidate this victory lest it fade. The wise remind us that if love is to survive, it must be exercised. We know this is true in our families and workplaces. It also is true in our country. It should be clear that every law we pass should foster love of country, and every parent, teacher, public figure, role model and hero should be a patriot who promotes patriotism in our youth and in our country. Again, all our heroes should be patriots; all our celebrities are not.

With Us or Against Us

We are clear that in terms of terrorism, you are either with us or against us. We should be just as clear with patriotism—you are either a patriot, one who supports and defends America, or you are not a patriot. The love of a patriot can be known only by the acts of a patriot.

The Bible teaches that there is a time for everything under the sun. Now is the time to enshrine patriotism in America, a time to denounce the anti-patriots, a time to expose the false patriots, a time to announce that we are ashamed to have them as countrymen.

The highest form of patriotism is service to our youth. No one is born a patriot; it must be taught. We should teach our children to be horrified by the awful offal of the counterfeit patriots and instill in them a love of America that alone can generate the sacrifices necessary to guarantee our freedoms.

4

Enshrined Patriotism Endangers America

Cecilia O'Leary and Tony Platt

Cecilia O'Leary, a history professor at California State University in Monterey Bay, is the author of To Die For: The Paradox of American Patriotism. *Tony Platt, a professor of social work at California State University in Sacramento, is the author of* The Child Savers: The Invention of Delinquency.

After the terrorist attacks of September 11, 2001, Americans embraced rituals and symbols that expressed a sense of national belonging. However, the Bush administration used this time of crisis to pass resolutions intended to enforce a narrow kind of patriotism among the nation's school children, including the requirement to recite the Pledge of Allegiance daily. History reveals that this pledge has too often been used to impose militarism and unquestioning obedience to authority. Furthermore, prescribed patriotism often leads to a fanatical nationalism, the suppression of dissent, and the persecution of minorities. Rather than participating in rote patriotic drills, students should be learning the art of debate and democratic participation.

In a matter of a few months, we have witnessed far-reaching changes in American global doctrines, the domestic economy and politics of government, and national security and criminal justice. Our focus in this essay is on shifts in the cultural politics of nationalism. During the flush years of an exuberant dot-com economy, being an American meant little more than the freedom to consume or visit Disneyland. But since the

Cecilia O'Leary and Tony Platt, "Pledging Allegiance: The Revival of Prescriptive Patriotism," *Social Justice*, vol. 28, Fall 2001, p. 41. Copyright © 2001 by the Crime and Social Justice Associates. Reproduced by permission.

September 11 [2001, terrorist] attacks, a resurgent patriotism is omnipresent and nowhere is it more on display than in our schools.

In October 2001, the Bush administration launched a series of initiatives aimed at prescribing patriotism among the nation's 52 million schoolchildren. Government officials urged students to take part in a mass recitation of the Pledge of Allegiance, and called upon veterans to teach "Lessons for Liberty." The House of Representatives voted 444-0 for the display of signs proclaiming "God Bless America" in the public schools. At the local level, the New York City Board of Education unanimously passed a resolution requiring all public schools to lead a daily pledge in the morning and at all school assemblies. "It's a small way to thank the heroes of 9/11," explained the Board's president. In Madison, Wisconsin, the School Board reversed its previous position and voted to allow schools to recite a daily Pledge of Allegiance and sing "The Star-Spangled Banner." Nebraska dusted off a 1949 state law requiring schools to devise curricula aimed at instilling a "love of liberty, justice, democracy and America . . . in the hearts and minds of the youth." And after years of futile attempts, a conservative, fringe organization in Orange County—Celebration USA Inc.—succeeded in synchronizing a nationwide recitation of the pledge at 2:00 P.M. eastern time on October 12th.

Imposing Allegiance

In the aftermath of September 11, people are hungry for social rituals and eager to communicate a deeper sense of national belonging. Yet this new wave of orchestrated patriotism is aimed at closing down debate and dissent through the imposition of a prescribed allegiance.

> *[A] new wave of orchestrated patriotism is aimed at closing down debate and dissent through the imposition of a prescribed allegiance.*

Rituals of patriotism were first institutionalized in the United States between the Civil War and World War I. At the end of the bloodiest civil war of the 19th century, the combatants left the battlefields for political, economic, and cultural arenas, where the struggle to make a nation continued with renewed intensity. In fact, many of the patriotic symbols and rituals that we now take for granted or think of as timeless were created during this period and emerged not from a harmonious, national consensus, but out of fiercely contested debates, even over the wording of the Pledge. Confronted by the dilemma that Americans are made, not born, educators and organizations, such as the Grand Army of the Republic, Women's Relief Corps, and Daughters of the American Republic, campaigned to transform schools, in George Balch's words, into a "mighty engine for the inculcation of patriotism."

Balch, a New York City teacher and Civil War veteran, wrote what is thought to be the first pledge to the flag in which students promised to "give our heads and our hearts to God and our Country! One nation! One language! One flag!" Balch intended the pledge to teach discipline and loyalty to the "human scum, cast on our shores by the tidal wave of a vast migration." In 1890, Balch published a primer for educators on *Methods for Teaching Patriotism in the Public Schools*, which called for the use of devotional rites of patriotism modeled along the lines of a catechism. "There is nothing which more impresses the youthful mind and excites its emotions," noted the West Point graduate, than the "observance of form."

> *The pledge [of allegiance], once imagined as a living principle of justice and liberty . . . quickly became suffused with militarism and obedience to authority.*

To commemorate the first celebration of Columbus Day in 1892 and in preparation for the grand opening of the Columbian Exposition in Chicago, the *Youth's Companion* magazine charged Francis Bellamy with writing a new pledge. Bellamy, a Christian socialist with a commitment to social reform, dismissed Balch's formula as a "pretty childish form of words, invented by an ex-military officer." He wanted a pledge that would resonate with American history and make students into active participants in a "social citizenry." For Bellamy, the notion of "allegiance" evoked the great call to union during the

Civil War and "one nation indivisible" recalled a phrase used by [Abraham] Lincoln. Bellamy was tempted to add the historic slogan of the French Revolution—"Liberty, Equality, Fraternity"—to the language of his pledge, but in the end he decided that this would be too much for people to accept. Instead, he settled for the final phrase, "with liberty and justice for all." This way, he reasoned, the pledge could be ideologically "applicable to either an individualistic or a socialistic state," a matter for future generations to decide.

> *Between the World Wars, campaigns for '100 percent Americanism' led to the persecution of thousands of Jehovah's Witnesses . . . when they refused to salute the flag.*

Bellamy's words—"I pledge allegiance to my flag and to the Republic for which it stands, one Nation indivisible, with liberty and justice for all"—were gradually adopted throughout the country. But the pledge, once imagined as a living principle of justice and liberty, perhaps even equality, quickly became suffused with militarism and obedience to authority. On Columbus Day, 1892, according to newspaper reports, children marched with "drilled precision" as "one army under the sacred flag."

Prescribed Patriotism

In the wake of the Spanish-American War, state-sanctioned rituals of patriotism became more common. In New York, the day after war was declared on April 29, 1898, the legislature instructed the state superintendent of public instruction to prepare "a program providing for a salute to the flag at the opening of each day of school." Daily rituals aimed at reaching children's hearts were backed up with new civics curriculums to secure their minds with heroic images of virile soldiers and the honor of dying for one's country. A typical children's primer published in 1903 taught, "B stood for battles" and Z for the "zeal that has carried us through/When fighting for justice/With the Red, White and Blue."

During World War I, Americanizers worried about dual allegiances and feared that Bellamy's pledge allowed cunning fifth-columnist immigrants to swear a secret loyalty to another country. To close this loophole, the words "my flag" were extended into "the flag of the United States." Many states now required students to salute the flag every day. In Chicago in 1916, an 11-year old African American student was arrested because he refused to respect a symbol that represented Jim Crow and lynching. "I am willing to salute the flag," Hubert Eaves explained, "as the flag salutes me."

> *At times of crisis . . . the most patriotic act of all is the unyielding defense of civil liberties, the right to dissent and equality before the law for all Americans.*

Meanwhile, Boy Scout troops across the country staged massive operettas in celebration of "America First," while vigilantes forced German Americans suspected of insufficient loyalty to kiss the flag. A judge, unable to reverse a lower court's decision to sentence a man to 20 years of hard labor for abusive language toward the flag, believed that the man was "more sinned against than sinning." The mob, he wrote in his opinion, had descended into the kind of "fanaticism" that fueled the "tortures of the Inquisition."

Between the World Wars, campaigns for "100 percent Americanism" led to the persecution of thousands of Jehovah's Witnesses and the expulsion of their children from school when they refused to salute the flag. What began as a movement to encourage loyalty to a nation "with liberty and justice for all" had deviated into the suppression of dissent and unquestioning homage to the flag.

In 1943, the U.S. Supreme Court ruled in *West Virginia State Board of Education v. Barnette* that an obligatory loyalty oath was unconstitutional, thus putting law on the side of any student who refuses to participate in patriotic or religious rituals. But even after the ruling, refusal to say the pledge took both courage and conviction.

The pledge remained unchanged until Flag Day, 1954, when President [Dwight] Eisenhower approved the addition of the constitutionally questionable phrase "under God" to differentiate this country from its godless Cold War antagonist.

The Purpose of Our Nation

In the wake of public opposition to the Vietnam War, educators were not inclined to impose rote patriotic drills on their students or to resurrect the slogan of "One country, one language, one flag," which guided the teaching of civics earlier in the century. Since the 1980s, many schools have slowly begun to adopt textbooks and develop curriculums that speak to the needs of a multiethnic, polyglot population living in an increasingly interrelated world. This is not the time to reverse this trend by reverting to form over substance and rote memorization over democratic participation.

"What of our purpose as a Nation?" pondered Francis Bellamy more than a century ago when he crafted his pledge. Our students today can better use their time debating this question than marching in lockstep loyalty. "At times of crisis," writes historian Eric Foner, "the most patriotic act of all is the unyielding defense of civil liberties, the right to dissent and equality before the law for all Americans."

5

The American Flag Has Become a Symbol of Inequality and Dominance

Kimberly Ridley

Kimberly Ridley is the editor of Hope, *a bimonthly journal.*

While the American flag should be an emblem of liberty and justice for all, today it often symbolizes discord, inequality, and the dominance of those in power. Americans are experiencing a crisis because they have lost sight of their deeper values and a sense of connectedness to others. Consequently, they are more prone to fear and manipulation, which makes it more difficult for them to believe that their actions and their votes can make a difference. Americans need to recognize that they are interdependent—connected to other peoples, other nations, other species—and the American flag should be reclaimed as a symbol of compassion, tolerance, community, and strength.

Our local Independence Day celebration is straight out of a Norman Rockwell painting. The centerpiece is the parade: a procession of gleaming fire trucks from several towns, followed by a half-dozen or so home-grown floats, kids on decorated bikes, uniformed Boy Scouts, an ancient calliope, and antique and not-so-antique cars bringing up the rear. The whole shebang winds its way to the town green for games and a chicken barbecue sponsored by the local Youth Corps.

There's much I love about this day—kids scrambling for candy flung from the floats, parents and grandparents parked in lawn chairs under the maples that shade the library lawn, the bake sales and rummage sales, the way locals and visitors mingle with ease. But a shadow hangs over this lovely little scene, and it's cast by the flag.

A Symbol of Divisiveness

Too often these days, the flag symbolizes divisiveness rather than democratic process in this country—"You're either with us or against us"—and domination rather than freedom abroad. It is in danger of becoming a symbol of privilege for a few instead of liberty and justice for all. This dishonors the sacrifices of veterans and the memory of those who died believing they were upholding America's highest ideals. As I see the flags waving on Independence Day, I feel more sad than proud. Sure, we're free from British rule. But forces far worse are colonizing our nation: ideologies built on selfishness and greed.

> *[The flag] is in danger of becoming a symbol of privilege for a few instead of liberty and justice for all.*

I love this country, but I fear for its future. How did a majority of voters come to elect lawmakers whose decisions so often defy our values of common sense, decency, and compassion? What does it mean that we let our elected officials grant our wealthier citizens an enormous tax cut while our poorer ones face excruciating need? What keeps most of us silent as this country spends more than *a billion dollars a day* on the military? How did we get so distracted from what truly matters and relinquish our voice as caring human beings?

A Crisis of Meaning

Our country is in crisis, but it's not about politics or the economy or homeland security. The crisis lives inside us, each one of us, and it's a crisis of meaning and connection. When we lose sight of our deeper values and ideals, and our connection to others, we're easy to frighten and manipulate. We're easy to deceive. We're easy to overwhelm and convince that our actions don't matter or our votes don't count.

I certainly feel this crisis in my own heart. Yet as painful as this struggle is, it's also what gives me hope. If our nation's crisis resides within us rather than outside us, we each have the power to do something about it. Which brings me back to the star-spangled parades marching down my Main Street and yours.

Independence in the sentimental sense of the word is obsolete. None of us, as nations or individuals, does anything alone. We are interdependent. We rely upon people from other countries—often paid poorly and treated worse—to grow and harvest much of our food, and make our clothes and myriad necessities. We need other human beings to love and feed us, to teach and heal us, and they need us to do the same for them. Our very lives depend on other species and the health of the Earth itself, its soil, water, and air.

This Fourth of July, and every day, for that matter, I want to celebrate interdependence: our life-sustaining connections with each other and the planet. When I look beyond all the flags at our little parade to see who's waving them, I see children I treasure, neighbors, strangers, human beings—all different, but sharing the same basic needs: love, community, tolerance, and compassion. Our lives, all lives, are connected, and we need to infuse our symbols and celebrations with this understanding. I'm not yet sure how to recapture our flag or reclaim our nation, but I think it begins with recognizing our humanity.

Interdependence is a gift, a pleasure, a responsibility. As we strengthen and celebrate our connections with one another, we all grow stronger. We get clear on the kind of life and world we want for ourselves and others, and we're suddenly very difficult to deceive, control, or intimidate. When we declare our interdependence, we stand a decent chance of shaping the future.

6

The American Flag Is a Symbol of Patriotism and Unity

Dave Desilets

Dave Desilets is managing editor of All Hands.

The American flag emblematizes hope, freedom, courage, and unity. In the weeks after the terrorist attacks of September 11, 2001, the U.S. flag was widely flown—embraced as a powerful symbol of democracy and sacrifice and representative of a unified stance in the face of adversity. As time passed, however, the American flag became less visible. Citizens of the United States should not become complacent about the state of their nation. They should continue to wave the flag as an expression of courage and unity.

If it can be said that something good came of [the terrorist attacks of September 11, 2001], it would have to be the renewed sense of national unity and patriotism that overwhelmed our country in the midst if its mourning and response. A powerful symbol of our singular stand during the aftermath was the United States Flag.

And as we recovered and responded, our national ensign was everywhere. It was erected amid the World Trade Center rubble by heroic New York City firefighters, draped over the Pentagon by proud volunteers, signed by its free people as a petition for democracy and independence and later flown above

Dave Desilets, "Does Your Flag Still Wave?" *All Hands*, June 2002, p. 48.

a newly freed Afghanistan.[1] It was stretched across ball fields, and in its most solemn duty, our flag covered bodies and coffins. It was cried upon, sung to, prayed under and embraced as the one common emblem this melting pot of a country— and of a world, could hold on to in a uniting gesture of understanding and care.

The Stars and Stripes

In a time of tragedy, our flag has been a bright beacon of hope and fortitude. Much like in the War of 1812, when rockets glared red in the perilous night sky over Baltimore harbor, and Francis Scott Key saw the next morning that our Star Spangled Banner was still there. The Stars and Stripes has valiantly carried our nation in its majestic ripple during the months following terror on its soil.

> **"***Maintaining our united stand could be simply accomplished by waving America's flag.***"**

Since September 11th, there have been many flag days. Every day it has flown, it has made the same strong statement of "united we stand" in a free and democratic country for which it tirelessly represents. And as time goes by, as we resume life's routine, as we fight a very long and hard battle against the evil of this world, one might ask if its citizens would tire of it?

Think back on your neighborhood in the weeks after the terrorist attacks. Flag after flag hung from porches and poles, windows and doors. Bumpers and buildings were adorned in red, white and blue. Children waved flags as they sang our national anthem. Our military saluted it during numerous ceremonies. Olympic athletes held it high. And gravesites were adorned with little stick flags. But [many] months later, are our nation's colors still as visible? And if not, why not?

In this particular war, one could argue that our flag has never been more visible as a symbol of pride and freedom. Then

1. In the fall of 2001, the United States led an invasion of Afghanistan to oust the ruling Taliban. The Taliban was aiding the terrorist group al Qaeda, believed responsible for the September 11, 2001, terrorist attacks on America.

again, ever since its early stripes and circle of stars, "Old Glory" has rallied its citizens through battles and victories, hardships and celebrations.

Because of its importance and national service, Flag Day, June 14th, was proclaimed by President Woodrow Wilson in 1916, and later signed by President Harry S. Truman as an Act of Congress in 1949. But the idea of properly recognizing our flag dates back to 1885, when a Wisconsin schoolteacher gathered students to celebrate a Flag Birthday. Through the following years of local commemorations, a national day of recognition was spawned. In 1996, then-President Bill Clinton expanded Flag Day to a week.

Prior to official declarations in a 1914 Flag Day address, then-Secretary of the Interior Franklin K. Lane summed up our national banner's role in a simple inspiration, "I am what you make me; nothing more. I swing before your eyes as a bright gleam of color, a symbol of yourself."

In times like these, it is said that we should not grow complacent in the matters of our country's business and welfare. Nor should our unity wane. Keeping the nation and the civilized world safe from terror may be a difficult and daunting task, but maintaining our united stand could be simply accomplished by waving America's flag.

Forever may it wave.

7

Left-Wing Dissent Is Patriotic

Peter Dreier and Dick Flacks

Peter Dreier teaches politics and public policy at Occidental College and is the coauthor of Place Matters: Metropolitics for the 21st Century. *Dick Flacks teaches sociology at the University of California in Santa Barbara and is the author of* Making History: The American Left and the American Mind.

While many people claim that left-wingers are anti-American and unpatriotic, history reveals just the opposite. From the nineteenth century up through the twenty-first century, progressive writers, artists, and thinkers have expressed a patriotism rooted in democratic values and the desire for equality, liberty, and social justice. For example, many items in America's patriotic repertoire—including the Pledge of Allegiance and the songs "America the Beautiful" and "This Land Is Your Land"—were written by progressives or Socialists. Left-wing patriots often express their love of America by opposing misguided government policies, jingoistic nationalism, and militarism.

Many Americans believe that the left is "antipatriotic" (and even anti-American), while the political right truly expresses the American spirit and reveres its symbols. Particularly since the late 1960s—when the movement against US intervention in Vietnam gained momentum—the terms "progressive" and "patriotism" have rarely been used in the same sentence, at least in the mainstream media. It has become conventional wisdom that conservatives wave the American flag while leftists burn it. Patriotic Americans display the flag on their homes; progressives turn it upside down to show contempt.

The Undermining of Dissent

Recent months have seen a dramatic increase in the number of Americans proudly displaying the Stars and Stripes on their cars, homes, businesses, T-shirts, caps, lapel pins and even tattoos. This outpouring of flag-waving signifies a variety of sentiments—from identification with the victims of the September 11 [2001, terrorist] attacks to support for the military's invasion of Afghanistan [in 2001 to topple the ruling Taliban]. But in our popular culture, displays of the American flag are—along with the very idea of "patriotism"—typically viewed as expressions of "conservative" politics. The patriotic fervor since September 11 has revitalized that belief and, as in other times, has given conservative politicos and pundits a handy means to undermine dissent and progressive initiatives.

A case in point: In Santa Barbara, California, progressive County Supervisor Gail Marshall is facing the possibility of a recall election fueled by right-wing forces opposed to her support for environmental regulation, affordable housing and labor unions. Because Marshall occupies the key swing seat on the five-member county board, Santa Barbara's conservative activists—funded by oil interests, agribusiness and land developers—have been trying to unseat her for years. They launched a recall campaign after Marshall refused to rubber-stamp a proposal to require the Pledge of Allegiance at meetings of one of her community advisory boards. Marshall said she wanted the board to discuss the idea, but her opponents—who made sure that TV camera crews were present at the meeting where the issue first surfaced—have turned her civil libertarian instincts into proof that she's hostile to public expressions of patriotism.

In TV ads and newsletters, Marshall's opponents . . . claim that her alleged reluctance to have the pledge recited was clear confirmation of their suspicion that she is a "socialist."

The Author of the Pledge of Allegiance

Ironically, the Pledge of Allegiance was written in 1892 by a leading Christian socialist, Francis Bellamy, who was fired from his Boston ministry for his sermons depicting Jesus as a socialist. Bellamy penned the Pledge of Allegiance for *Youth's Com-*

panion, a magazine for young people published in Boston with a circulation of about 500,000.

A few years earlier, the magazine had sponsored a largely successful campaign to sell American flags to public schools. In 1891 the magazine hired Bellamy—whose first cousin Edward Bellamy was the famous socialist author of the utopian novel *Looking Backward*—to organize a public relations campaign to celebrate the 400th anniversary of Christopher Columbus's discovery of America by promoting use of the flag in public schools. Bellamy gained the support of the National Education Association, along with President Benjamin Harrison and Congress, for a national ritual observance in the schools, and he wrote the Pledge of Allegiance as part of the program's flag salute ceremony.

Bellamy thought such an event would be a powerful expression on behalf of free public education. Moreover, he wanted all the schoolchildren of America to recite the pledge at the same moment. He hoped the pledge would promote a moral vision to counter the individualism embodied in capitalism and expressed in the climate of the Gilded Age, with its robber barons and exploitation of workers. Bellamy intended the line "One nation indivisible with liberty and justice for all" to express a more collective and egalitarian vision of America.

Bellamy's view that unbridled capitalism, materialism and individualism betrayed America's promise was widely shared in the nineteenth and twentieth centuries. Many American radicals and progressive reformers proudly asserted their patriotism. To them, America stood for basic democratic values—economic and social equality, mass participation in politics, free speech and civil liberties, elimination of the second-class citizenship of women and racial minorities, a welcome mat for the world's oppressed people. The reality of corporate power, right-wing xenophobia and social injustice only fueled progressives' allegiance to these principles and the struggle to achieve them.

Left-Wing Patriotism

Most Americans are unaware that much of our patriotic culture—including many of the leading icons and symbols of American identity—was created by artists and writers of decidedly left-wing and even socialist sympathies. A look at the songs sung at post-9/11 patriotic tribute events and that appear on the various patriotic compilation albums, or the clips incorporated into film shorts celebrating the "American spirit,"

reveals that the preponderance of these originated in the forgotten tradition of left-wing patriotism.

Begin with the lines inscribed on the Statue of Liberty:
"Give me your tired, your poor/Your huddled masses yearning
to breathe free." Emma Lazarus was a poet of considerable rep-
utation in her day, a well-known figure in literary circles. She
was a strong supporter of Henry George and his "socialistic"
single-tax program, and a friend of William Morris, a leading
British socialist. Her welcome to the "wretched refuse" of the
earth, written in 1883, was an effort to project an inclusive and
egalitarian definition of the American dream.

> *Most Americans are unaware that much of
> our patriotic culture . . . was created by artists and
> writers of decidedly left-wing and even socialist
> sympathies.*

The words to "America the Beautiful" were written in 1893
by Katharine Lee Bates, a professor of English at Wellesley College. Bates was an accomplished and published poet, whose
book *America the Beautiful and Other Poems* includes a sequence
of poems expressing outrage at US imperialism in the Philip-
pines. Indeed, Bates identified with the anti-imperialist movement of her day and was part of progressive reform circles in
the Boston area concerned about labor rights, urban slums and
women's suffrage. She was also an ardent feminist, and for
decades lived with and loved her Wellesley colleague Katharine
Coman, an economist and social activist. "America the Beautiful" not only speaks to the beauty of the American continent
but also reflects her view that US imperialism undermines the
nation's core values of freedom and liberty. The poem's final
words—"and crown thy good with brotherhood, from sea to
shining sea"—are an appeal for social justice rather than the
pursuit of wealth.

The Unofficial National Anthem

Many Americans consider Woody Guthrie's song "This Land Is
Your Land," penned in 1940, to be our unofficial national anthem. Guthrie was a radical with strong ties to the Communist

Party. He was inspired to write the song as an answer to Irving Berlin's popular "God Bless America," which he thought failed to recognize that it was the "people" to whom America belonged. The words to "This Land Is Your Land" reflect Guthrie's fusion of patriotism, support for the underdog and class struggle. In this song Guthrie celebrates America's natural beauty and bounty but criticizes the country for its failure to share its riches, reflected in the song's last and least-known verse:

> One bright sunny morning in the shadow
> of the steeple
> By the relief office I saw my people.
> As they stood hungry I stood there
> wondering
> If this land was made for you and me.

Guthrie was not alone in combining patriotism and radicalism during the Depression and World War II. In this period, many American composers, novelists, artists and playwrights engaged in similar projects. In the early 1930s, for example, a group of young composers and musicians—including Marc Blitzstein (author of the musical "The Cradle Will Rock"), Charles Seeger (a well-known composer and musicologist, and father of folk singer Pete Seeger) and Aaron Copland—formed the "composers' collective" to write music that would serve the cause of the working class. They turned to American roots and folk music for inspiration. Many of their compositions—including Copland's "Fanfare for the Common Man" and "Lincoln Portrait"—are now patriotic musical standards, regularly performed at major civic events.

> *American progressives [continue] . . . to fuse their love of country with their opposition to the national government's policies.*

Earl Robinson was a member of the composers' collective who pioneered the effort to combine patriotism and progressivism. In 1939 he teamed with lyricist John La Touche to write "Ballad for Americans," which was performed on the CBS radio network by Paul Robeson, accompanied by chorus and orchestra. This eleven-minute cantata provided a musical review of

American history, depicted as a struggle between the "nobodies who are everybody" and an elite that fails to understand the real, democratic essence of America.

Robeson, at the time one of the best-known performers on the world stage, became, through this work, a voice of America. Broadcasts and recordings of "Ballad for Americans" (by Bing Crosby as well as Robeson) were immensely popular. In the summer of 1940, it was performed at the national conventions of both the Republican and Communist parties. The work soon became a staple in school choral performances, but it was literally ripped out of many public school songbooks after Robinson and Robeson were identified with the radical left and blacklisted during the McCarthy period.[1] Since then, however, "Ballad for Americans" has been periodically revived, notably during the bicentennial celebration in 1976, when a number of pop and country singers performed it in concerts and on TV.

> *[Bruce] Springsteen has coupled his anger at injustice with his belief in the nation's promise.*

During World War II, with lyricist Lewis Allen, Robinson co-wrote another patriotic hit, "The House I Live In." Its lyrics asked, and then answered, the question posed in the first line of the song, "What is America to me?" The song evokes America as a place where all races can live freely, where one can speak one's mind, where the cities as well as the natural landscapes are beautiful. The song was made a hit by Frank Sinatra in 1945. Sinatra also starred in an Oscar-winning movie short—written by Albert Maltz, later one of the Hollywood Ten—in which he sang "The House I Live In" to challenge bigotry, represented in the movie by a gang of kids who rough up a Jewish boy.

"The House I Live In," like "Ballad for Americans," was exceedingly popular for several years but became controversial during the McCarthy period and has largely disappeared from

---

1. This refers to a time during the Cold War in the 1950s when Senator Joe McCarthy publicly accused numerous American artists and activists of being Communists and, therefore, disloyal to their country.

public consciousness. Its co-author, Lewis Allen, was actually Abel Meeropol, a high school teacher who also penned "Strange Fruit," the anti-lynching song made famous by Billie Holiday. In the 1950s Meeropol and his wife adopted the sons of Julius and Ethel Rosenberg after their parents were executed as atom spies. Despite this, Sinatra kept the song in his repertoire. Perhaps the most astonishing performance of "The House I Live In" was at the nationally televised commemoration of the centenary of the Statue of Liberty in 1986, when Sinatra sang it as the finale to the program, with President Ronald Reagan and his wife, Nancy Reagan, sitting directly in front of him.

> *Progressives [express] a patriotism rooted in democratic values and consciously aimed at challenging jingoism and 'my country, right or wrong' thinking.*

Only a handful of Americans could have grasped the political irony of that moment: Sinatra performing a patriotic anthem written by blacklisted writers to a President who, as head of the Screen Actors Guild in the 1950s, helped create Hollywood's purge of radicals. Sinatra's own left-wing (and nearly blacklisted) past, and the history of the song itself, have been obliterated from public memory.

The 1960s

Even during the 1960s, American progressives continued to seek ways to fuse their love of country with their opposition to the national government's policies. The March on Washington in 1963 gathered at the Lincoln Memorial, where Martin Luther King Jr. famously quoted the words to "My Country 'Tis of Thee." Phil Ochs, then part of a new generation of politically conscious singer-songwriters who emerged during the 1960s, wrote an anthem in the Guthrie vein, "Power and Glory," which coupled love of country with a strong plea for justice and equality. Interestingly, this song later became part of the repertoire of the US Army band. And in 1968, in a famous antiwar speech on the steps of the Capitol, Norman Thomas, the aging leader of the Socialist Party, proclaimed, "I come to cleanse the American flag, not burn it."

In recent decades, Bruce Springsteen has most closely followed in the Guthrie tradition. From "Born in the USA," to his songs about Tom Joad (the militant protagonist in John Steinbeck's *Grapes of Wrath*), to his recent anthem for the victims of the September 11 tragedy ("My City of Ruins"), whom he urges to "come on rise up!" Springsteen has championed the downtrodden while challenging America to live up to its ideals. Indeed, by performing both "Born in the USA" and "Land of Hope and Dreams" at benefits for the families of World Trade Center casualties, Springsteen has coupled his anger at injustice with his belief in the nation's promise.

Challenging Jingoism

In each major period of twentieth-century history—the Progressive era, the Depression, World War II and the postwar era—American radicals and progressives expressed a patriotism rooted in democratic values and consciously aimed at challenging jingoism and "my country, right or wrong" thinking. Every day, millions of Americans pledge allegiance to the flag, sing "America the Beautiful" and "This Land Is Your Land," and memorize the words on the Statue of Liberty without knowing the names of their authors, their political inspiration or the historical context in which they were written.

The progressive authors of much of America's patriotic iconography rejected blind nationalism, militaristic drumbeating and sheeplike conformism. So it would be a dire mistake to allow, by default, jingoism to become synonymous with patriotism and the American spirit. Throughout our nation's history, radicals and reformers have viewed their movements as profoundly patriotic. They have believed that America's core claims—fairness, equality, freedom, justice—were their own. In the midst of current patriotic exuberance both authentic and manipulated, then, it is useful to recall the forgotten cultural legacy of the left. We need to ask, once again, "What is America to us?"

8

Left-Wing Dissent Is Not Patriotic

Don Feder

Nationally syndicated columnist Don Feder is an editorial writer for the Boston Herald *and the author of* A Jewish Conservative Looks at Pagan America.

Patriotism is under attack by a left-wing cabal of historical revisionists, multiculturalists, educators, artists, and politicians. The leaders of the left—who occupy influential posts in schools and in the media—express contempt for America's heritage and portray the nation as oppressive, greedy, and inhumane. As a result, young Americans often fail to appreciate their country's great past and treasured ideals. Patriots must defend America from left-wing attacks if they want to ensure the survival of their country.

Dec. 7 [2001] marks the 60th anniversary of the United States' entry in to World War II. On May 25, Touchstone Pictures . . . releases the movie *Pearl Harbor*, in tribute to what many have called the "Greatest Generation."

Those who served their country so nobly from 1941 to 1945 knew what they were fighting for—their homes and families to be sure, but also something greater.

They were fighting for a vision of humanity and its relation to government embodied in a document signed in Philadelphia in 1776, for the more perfect union enunciated in the same city in 1787 and for the tall, gaunt figure who became a martyr to the preservation of the union in 1865. They were inspired by the heroism associated with names such as George Washington,

Andrew Jackson and Teddy Roosevelt. They fought to preserve the ideals of equality before the law, liberty, justice and decency.

Those young men paid again for our freedom in blood, terror and pain in places with names such as Normandy, the Bulge, Guadalcanal and Iwo Jima, in a conflict in which there were more than 1 million American casualties and 440 Medals of Honor awarded.

A Sense of Duty

James Bradley, author of *Flags of Our Fathers*, is the son of one of the Marines who raised the Stars and Stripes atop Iwo Jima's Mount Suribachi, immortalized in the famous photograph. After his father's death, Bradley learned that days before the flag raising his corpsman father had been awarded the Navy Cross. The writer explained that his father received the Navy's second-highest decoration after "a shell drove hot shrapnel into his legs, hips and feet. His pants were shredded and soaked with blood. But eyewitnesses said he would not tend his own wounds as he continued to care for those around him."

Only a sense of duty and a deep love of country can inspire such devotion. When the United States goes to war again, will other young Americans be instilled with the same spirit?

Not if we continue on our current course. Patriotism is dying a slow death, poisoned by revisionists, multiculturalists, advocates of hyphenated identity and an elite that disparages our history and heritage and rejects our ideals (a worldview that used to be called "the American way").

Thanks to their ceaseless efforts, young Americans no longer learn their history, celebrate their heroes or grasp their nation's uniqueness.

Teaching Contempt for the Past

In a December 1999 study conducted by the Center for Survey Research and Analysis at the University of Connecticut, only 23 percent of seniors at 55 of the nation's most prestigious colleges and universities correctly identified James Madison as the principal framer of the Constitution. Almost 80 percent earned a grade of D or F on a 34-question, high-school-level, American history test.

While it's true that not one of these schools has an American history requirement, the problem originates with public education. For instance, James C. Rees, the overseer of Washington's estate at Mount Vernon, discloses, "George Washington has been virtually eliminated from elementary-school textbooks." Washington—the indispensable man in the War for Independence, who chaired the Constitutional Convention, shaped the office of president and guided the republic for the first quarter-century of its existence—purged from grade-school textbooks? How can this be, even in an age given to citing patriotism as a last refuge of scoundrels or a synonym for jingoism?

> *Patriotism is dying a slow death, poisoned by revisionists, multiculturalists, [and] advocates of hyphenated identity.*

Apparently, American schoolchildren are too busy studying ancient Incas and Ibo tribesmen and paying homage to the icons of feminism and racial identity to bother with the story of the father of their country. Or could the omission be intentional?

Our institutions have been turned against us. Hollywood, academia, museums and the news media all teach contempt for our past. In movies such as *Platoon* and *Casualties of War* the entertainment industry portrayed the Americans who stemmed the communist advance in Southeast Asia as baby killers, addicts, rapists and degenerates. We've gone from Sergeant York to visions of noncommissioned officers with necklaces of human ears.

In the 1970s even the movie Western, a cinematic staple since the silent-film era, was replaced by the anti-Western—movies depicting pioneers, settlers, cowboys and soldiers as thieves, thugs and spoilers. This is best illustrated by *Dances With Wolves*, with its saintly, environmentally correct Indians and its crude, barbaric cavalry men. There's no more effective way to kill national pride than to convince a people that their past is a chronicle of crimes against humanity.

Left-Wing Excesses

Perhaps the epitome of establishment anti-Americanism were left-wing excesses at the taxpayer-supported Smithsonian Institution, where radicals ran the shows through most of the 1990s.

After its 1991 art exhibit, "The West as America," which presented our westward expansion as a tale of genocide, ecocide and unrestrained avarice, the Smithsonian hit its stride with a 1995 exhibit on the end of World War II in the Pacific.

Designed around a display of the fuselage of the *Enola Gay* (the B-29 bomber that dropped the atomic bomb on Hiroshima), as originally envisioned, the exhibit presented imperial Japan as a land of gentle souls fighting cultural annihilation and the United States as a nation of brutes bent on bloody revenge. The initial script intoned: "For most Americans this . . . was a war of vengeance. For most Japanese it was a war to defend their unique cultures against Western imperialism." The rape of Nanking, the extraordinarily brutal occupation of East Asia, the bombing of Pearl Harbor, the Bataan death march, the starvation and cruelties visited upon Allied prisoners of war and a demonstrated commitment to defend the home islands to the last civilian, all were shoved down a memory hole.

> *There's no more effective way to kill national pride than to convince a people that their past is a chronicle of crimes against humanity.*

An outcry from veterans groups caused a modification of the exhibit. But there was never an acknowledgement from the curators and historians associated with this travesty that there was something grotesque about an institution charged with telling America's story using its public resources to defame the United States.

A Jaundiced View of History

Then came the National History Standards, part of then-president Bill Clinton's "Goals 2000" education program. Intended to serve as a model for teaching American history, the standards exaggerated the dark side of our national saga while downplaying our glory. Discussions of the Ku Klux Klan were suggested on no fewer than 17 occasions. Sen. Joe McCarthy came up for classroom discussion 19 times. Noble souls such as Robert E. Lee and Thomas Edison totally were ignored, as was the Constitutional Convention.

So jaundiced was this view of American history that the standards were denounced in the Senate by a vote of 99 to 1. While less dismal, the revised standards were still deeply flawed, according to Vice President Dick Cheney's wife, Lynne, former head of the National Endowment for the Humanities, the agency that funded them.

> *The assault on patriotism is orchestrated by the left from its commanding heights in the nation's culture.*

Efforts to inculcate an appreciation for America are met with implacable hostility by spokesmen for group loyalty. For 14 years, New Jersey state Sen. Gerald Cardinale has championed legislation to require the state's schoolchildren to recite certain portions of the Declaration of Independence each day. When Cardinale's bill was debated in February 2000, state Sen. William Bryant deflected a vote by arguing that such a requirement would insult African-American students because their ancestors were slaves when the document was written and its author, Thomas Jefferson, was a slave owner. By the same logic, black litigants should never cite the First Amendment because their progenitors were in bondage when the Bill of Rights was ratified and Madison wasn't exactly an abolitionist.

Attacking Patriotism

If the Declaration of Independence won't serve as a common bond for our diverse people, what will? The truth is that those who make such arguments don't want us to have common bonds.

The assault on patriotism is orchestrated by the left from its commanding heights in the nation's culture. Its leaders learned to loathe America during the 1960s, when the United States was presented as an imperialist, racist power—a land of greed, oppression and environmental rape. The protesters of the "New Left" (Marxism with shaggy hair and a scraggly beard) became the authors, educators, editors, scriptwriters and politicians of the 1990s. One of them even made it to the White House.

Subconsciously, their hatred for America is based on the

public's rejection of their egalitarian dogma, on the unwilling-ness of ordinary Americans to embrace a collectivism of race (where nonwhites become an ersatz proletariat) and on this na-tion's long-standing opposition to communism, which the left couldn't help feeling was a finer thing than democratic capi-talism, if at times misguided.

Hence the constant effort to tear America down—to lie about our past, debunk our heroes, malign our international in-tentions, spread paranoia about the so-called military-industrial complex and sneer at patriotism as a mindless attachment of the ignorant masses, which, if left unchecked, will lead to xeno-phobia, militarism and the crushing of dissent.

> *[Leftist] attacks on America always come in the guise of objectivity, . . . inclusion and a cleansing confession of historical wrongs.*

The left's premises will not stand up to scrutiny, which is why it is crucial that leftists never give the game away by re-vealing their true motives. Thus attacks on America always come in the guise of objectivity (seeing the past as it "really was"), inclusion and a cleansing confession of historical wrongs.

America's detractors are sublimely unconcerned about their success at making it impossible to defend this nation. In their estimation, external enemies exist only in our imaginations. Why should it be necessary to inspire our citizens to sacrifice to build America? Isn't that project over? Doesn't any further expansion threaten the environment and deny other people their rightful share of the Earth's resources?

What's So Bad About America?

But if their vision of our past and indictment of our present is correct, how did we go from colonial backwater to pre-eminent power in less than 200 years from our founding?

If our economic system is so deeply flawed, how did we be-come the great economic engine of the 20th century, turning out invention after marvelous invention, creating a tide of prosperity that lifted boats around the world? If our values are so ignoble, how is it that America defeated the monstrous evil of the past century's twin "isms"? If our political institutions are as corrupt as they say, then how did our republic become a model for developing nations? If America has no inherent virtue, why do more than half of the world's immigrants end up on our doorsteps?

Is America really so hard to love? Despite their constant carping, few of her critics voluntarily choose expatriation. It is up to those of us who still see her clearly to raise the standard, and—like the first patriots—to pledge our lives, fortunes and sacred honor to her defense.

In the course of history, America is unique, and we are very much in danger of losing her. Only love of country—not mindless flag-waving but a sincere devotion born of an appreciation for America's greatness—will bind together this diverse people across a sprawling land and give us the fortitude to meet this century's challenges as the Greatest Generation met theirs.

9

Christians Must Reject Patriotism

Stanley Hauerwas

Stanley Hauerwas is a professor of theological ethics at Duke University in Durham, North Carolina. He is also the author of several books, including Peaceable Kingdom, Resident Alien, *and* Community of Character.

Christianity requires the observance of pacifism and nonviolence because Jesus Christ chose to die on the cross rather than engage in violence to redeem the world. Moreover, a Christian's primary loyalty is to God, not to nation. Christians must therefore reject patriotism—especially when patriotism is expressed through militarism and war. In doing so, Christians exhibit Christlike love and a humility that presents alternatives to a world constrained by hopelessness and the fear of death.

I am a Christian pacifist. I would not be a pacifist if I were not a Christian, and I find it difficult to understand how one can be a Christian without being a pacifist.

Yet I never really wanted to be a pacifist. I first believed [Christian theologian] Reinhold Niebuhr when he insisted that if you desire justice, you had better be ready to kill someone along the way. But John Howard Yoder, in his extraordinary book *The Politics of Jesus,* convinced me that at the heart of Christian faith is the conviction that Christ chose to die on the cross rather than achieve the world's redemption through violence. The defeat of death through resurrection makes it both possible and necessary

Stanley Hauerwas, "Nonviolence and the War Without End: The Current War Challenges Christians to Grasp More Deeply than Ever the Violence at the Heart of Our Identity and Our Vocation," *South Atlantic Quarterly,* vol. 101, Spring 2002, pp. 425–33. Copyright © 2002 by Duke University Press. All rights reserved. Reproduced by permission.

that Christians live nonviolently in a world of violence.

In short, Christians choose nonviolence not because we believe it is a strategy to rid the world of war, but rather because faithful followers of Christ in a world of war cannot imagine being anything other than nonviolent. I am a pacifist because I believe nonviolence is a necessary condition for a politics not based on death or determined by the fear of death.

The First Loyalty Is to God

When I first declared I was a pacifist, I vaguely realized that this conviction might have some serious consequences. To be nonviolent might even change my life. I quit singing "The Star Spangled Banner"—a small reminder that my first loyalty is not to the United States but to God and God's church.

It never crossed my mind that such small acts might over the years make my response to [the terrorist attacks of] September 11, 2001, quite different from that of the good people who sing "God Bless America." That difference, moreover, haunts me. My father was a brick-layer and a good American. He worked hard all his life and hoped his work would not only support his family but make some contribution to our common life. Although my family was never militarized, it was composed of Texans who strived to be "good Americans." For most of my life I too was a good American, assuming that I owed much to the society that enabled me, the son of a bricklayer, to get a doctoral degree at Yale.

> *Christ chose to die on the cross rather than achieve the world's redemption through violence.*

Because I am pacifist, the American "we" will never be my "me." But to be alienated from the American "we" is not easy.

I found I did not share the reaction of most Americans to the destruction of the World Trade Center and the subsequent war. . . . Some have suggested that pacifists should have nothing to say about how events have unfolded since September 11. These voices argue that those who oppose the use of military force have no legitimate place in the discussion of how such force is used. To them, pacifism is politically detached and ir-relevant. That is not the kind of pacifism I represent.

Disavowing "Natural" Patriotism

When I refused to join the patriotic bandwagon to war, a friend accused me of disdaining all "natural loyalties" that bind us to-gether as human beings, even submitting such loyalties to a harsh and unforgiving standard. I wondered if he was right: Do I speak as a solitary individual, failing to acknowledge that our lives are interwoven with the lives of others—those who have gone before, those among whom we live, those with whom we identify, and those with whom we are in Christian commu-nion? Do I refuse to recognize that my life is made possible by the gifts of others? Do I forsake all forms of patriotism, failing to acknowledge that we as a people are better off because of the sacrifices that were made in World War II and other wars?

If you call patriotism "natural," I certainly do disavow that connection. Such a disavowal, I hope, does not mean that I am unattentive to the gifts I have received from past and present neighbors.

I pointed out to my friend that I assumed he also disdained some "natural loyalties," because he too is a Christian. After all, he had his children baptized. The "natural love" between par-ents and children is surely reconfigured when children are bap-tized into the death and resurrection of Christ. As Paul writes: "Do you not know that all of us who have been baptized into Christ Jesus were baptized into his death? Therefore we have been buried with him by baptism into death, so that, just as Christ was raised from the dead by the glory of God, so we too might walk in the newness of life. For if we have been united with him in a death like his, we will certainly be united with him in a resurrection like his" (Rom. 6:3–5).

Many Christians tend to focus on being united with Christ in his resurrection, thereby forgetting that we are also united with him in his death. Baptism, therefore, means that we must be ready to die, indeed have our children die, rather than be-tray the gospel.

The Uses of War

Immediately after the September 11 attacks, the nation reeled in disbelief and stunned silence. Finally, George W. Bush broke the silence with the words, "We are at war."

Bush's words were magic, necessary to reclaim the everyday. War is such normalizing discourse. Americans know war. Ironically, the notion of war made us feel safe at a time when we were terrified. One way we could go on with our lives was to find someone against whom to retaliate.

In the ensuing weeks, our leaders then asked us to engage in a second normalizing discourse. As U.S. businesses experienced economic setbacks from a grieving nation that had slacked on its consumer habit, we were told to shop.

A year later, we [were] still at war. There is no evidence that terrorism is on the wane—in fact, our government continually stokes fears of new imminent attacks and rogue nations.

The United States is a country that lives off the moral capital of our wars. The very fact that we can and do go to war is a moral necessity for a nation of consumers. War makes clear we must believe in something even if we are not sure what that something is, except that we are sure it is somehow related to the "American way of life."

> *My first loyalty is not to the United States but to God and God's church.*

With the ebbing of the Cold War, the United States was disoriented. Our "twilight struggle" with the evil empire gave us a moral coherence, a common purpose and meaning: defeating the threat of communism. But then the Soviet Union collapsed, depriving us of that coherence. How could the United States make sense of what it means to be "a people" without a common enemy?

Now, we can fight the war against terrorism. We can kill—something we are very good at, though we often fail to acknowledge how accomplished we are at it.

Furthermore, the war on terrorism is the best kind of war, because it is a war without end. The United States gets to have it any way it wants. It decides who counts and does not count as a terrorist. Some that are captured are prisoners of war; some are detainees. Some nations that violate human rights are allies in the noble cause; others are part of an axis of evil. When you are the biggest kid on the block, you can say whatever you want.

A nation at war has no time for the poor, no space to worry about the extraordinary inequities that constitute this society or about those parts of the world ravaged by hunger and genocide. Everything—civil liberties, due process, the protection of the law—must be subordinated to the one great moral enterprise of winning the unending war against terrorism.

The Witness of the Church

The war goes on. But so must the witness of the church. It is urgent that we reflect critically on the social, political, and cultural dimensions feeding this current convulsion of militarism and violence. But it is just as urgent to reflect on how these dangerous times call us as Christians to a deeper understanding of what it means to be a people formed by the good news of Jesus.

U.S. imperialism, often celebrated as the new globalism, is a frightening power—not only because of the harm such power inflicts on the innocent, but because it is difficult to imagine alternatives. In a world marred by terrorism, pacifists are often challenged: "How would you respond? What alternatives do you have to bombing Afghanistan?"[1]

My only response is that Christians do not have a foreign policy. We have something better: a church constituted by people who would rather die than kill.

Christians are not called to be heroes or shoppers. We are called to be holy. We do not think holiness is an individual achievement, but rather a set of practices to sustain a people who refuse to have their lives determined by the fear and denial of death. We believe that by so living, we offer our sisters and brothers an alternative to all politics based on the denial of death. We are acutely aware that we seldom are faithful to the gifts God has given us, but we hope the confession of our sins is a sign of hope in a world without hope.

Christian Nonviolence

Mark and Louise Zwick, founders of the Houston Catholic Worker House of Hospitality, rightly observe that the drama of our times is the split between the gospel and our culture. But

---

1. In the fall of 2001, the United States led a coalition to invade Afghanistan and topple the ruling Taliban. The Taliban was aiding al Qaeda, the terrorists responsible for the September 11, 2001, terrorist attacks.

they remind us: "One does not free persons by detaching them from the bonds that paralyze them; one flees persons by attaching them to their destiny." Christian nonviolence cannot and must not be understood as a position that is no more than being "against violence." If our pacifism is no more than "not violence," it betrays the form of life to which Christians have been called by Christ.

Christian nonviolence is no less than the very form and character of life to which we are called by Christ. It is but another name for the friendship we believe God has made possible, a friendship that constitutes the alternative to the violence that grips our lives and our world.

Do we, as pacifists and people rooted in and formed by nonviolence, have a response to terrorism? I believe we do. Our response is to continue living in a manner that witnesses to our belief that the world was not changed on September 11, 2001. The world was changed during the celebration of a Passover in A.D. 33.

The witness is more than political protest, as necessary as protest might be. That witness is incarnated in the daily life of a people who live out, humbly and imperfectly, this friendship of God.

Jesus did not come to make us safe. Rather, he came to make us disciples, citizens of a new age, a reign of surprise. God has given us the time and the imagination to respond to September 11 with what Jean Vanier terms "small acts of beauty and tenderness." These, if done with humility and confidence, "will bring unity to the world and break the chain of violence."

In fact, this may be the gift—certainly the challenge—of this war without end. We may be forced to claim our true loyalties as we never have before. We may come to grasp the fullness of our identity as a baptized people committed to and humbly seeking to live out a nonviolent life. In so doing, we will be drawn into the heart of a peace without end. And we may, with God's grace, draw the world with us.

10
Christians Make the Best Patriots

Peter C. Meilaender

Peter C. Meilaender is an assistant professor of political science at Houghton College in New York State.

Christians have often been questioned about their national allegiances because their beliefs emphasize the rewards of eternal life rather than earthly life. Their devotion to God and to a promised land in the afterlife seems to contradict any loyalty to a country. But Christians, like most other citizens, love their country because it is their home. And in a similar way that parents love their children, they love their country because it is what they have been given—not because it meets some perfect ideal of goodness or justice. While Christians may strive to make their country a better place, they accept it as a gift from God, faults and all. Christians, therefore, make wonderful patriots because they love their country without demanding that it become perfect to earn their loyalty.

There is always a danger of intense love destroying what I might call the "polyphony" of life. What I mean is that God requires that we should love him eternally with our whole hearts, yet not so as to compromise or diminish our earthly affections, but as a kind of cantus firmus to which the other melodies of lip provide the counterpoint. Earthly affection is one of these contrapuntal themes, a theme which enjoys an autonomy of its own. . . . Where the ground bass is firm and clear,

*there is nothing to stop the counterpoint from being de-
veloped to the utmost of its limits.*

—Dietrich Bonhoeffer,
Letters and Papers from Prison

Following the terrorist attacks of September 11 [2001], patriotism, for the first time in a long time, became fashionable
in America once again. This should prompt reflection among
Christians, for the world has always doubted whether Christians—who, after all, like to sing such hymns as "I'm but a
stranger here, heav'n is my home"—can really share the love of
country felt by other citizens. Even as reliable a commentator
as Walter Berns, in his recent book *Making Patriots*, attributes
something of this doubt to the American Founders themselves,
who, though not hostile to religion, deliberately set up a system in which "we are first of all citizens, and only secondarily
Christians, Jews, Muslims, or of any other religious persua-
sion." If many Christians, Jews, and Muslims are likely to disagree with Berns on this point, that only serves to emphasize
the dilemma. Nor is the dilemma merely theoretical, for it is a
hard fact of political life that the state needs citizens who feel
at least some love for their country. Periods of crisis like the present remind us, often tragically, that our security and freedom
ultimately rest upon the willingness of citizens to fight and
possibly to die for their country should the need arise. It is
therefore of some importance to consider why we, as citizens,
might come to feel the love of country that the state so ur-
gently requires.

> *Our security and freedom ultimately rest upon
the willingness of citizens to fight and possibly to
die for their country should the need arise.*

For if it is clear that the state requires it, it is less obvious
that we can be expected to feel it. Indeed, the problem of how
to inspire love of country has been one of the enduring ques-
tions of political thought. Plato emphasized this difficulty in
the *Republic*, where Socrates proposes that the only way to ensure the loyalty of citizens is to tell them what he calls a "noble lie": that they have all been born from the earth and are

thus, in a literal sense, blood relatives not only of each other, but also of the very land they inhabit. The city can rest secure in the love of its members, Socrates suggests, only by pretending that it is as natural as the family, that fellow citizens are as intimately related as brothers and sisters, and that the land itself is their common mother.

> *Most of us, most of the time, probably love our country less because it is good than simply because it is ours.*

This difficulty is even more pronounced in the theory of liberalism that forms the basis for our own political system. Plato, after all, described a Greek city-state that actively sought to mold virtuous citizens and to sustain the good life for human beings. Such a city, aiming to provide goods nobler than mere self-preservation, could plausibly ask citizens to die on its behalf. But liberalism abandons such grand political pretensions and settles for a state that merely protects the individual rights of fundamentally self-interested people. This is evident in the standard liberal model of the social contract. On this model, government arises from the voluntary agreement of individuals to submit to a common authority. They are willing to do so because government helps protect the things about which they care most—their lives, their liberty, their property. But if I think of political society in these terms, as simply a useful means for protecting my private, personal interests, what could possibly motivate me to fight, and perhaps die, for my country? Why would I stand fast on the front lines in the face of enemy fire? It is hard to know why a person whose driving motivation is the desire to preserve his life, liberty, and property would ever want to make a deal that might require his death. After all, if you join the state only to preserve your life, then a state that asks you to die for it is a pretty bad bargain.

Love of country has proved a special problem not only for liberals, but also for Christians. Roman Catholics in particular have frequently been viewed as unreliable and potentially subversive subjects because of their loyalty to Rome. Such suspicion of Catholics has continued even as a quite recent phenomenon. Many will remember, for example, John F. Kennedy's famous speech before the Greater Houston Ministerial Association in 1960, promising that if elected he would not take orders from the Vatican. Much earlier, the philosopher Jean-Jacques Rousseau, anxious that citizens should be united and share a single will, criticized Catholicism for giving them "two legislative orders, two rulers, two homelands, and put[ting] them under two contradictory obligations." Even Locke, arguing for religious toleration, conceded that not every group could be tolerated: "That Church can have no right to be tolerated by the Magistrate, which is constituted upon such a bottom that all those who enter into it do thereby, ipso facto, deliver themselves up to the Protection and Service of another Prince"—an exception aimed, presumably, at Catholics loyal to the Pope.

> **" *Loyalty based upon a country's goodness or justice is potentially a very dangerous thing.* "**

But the blunt, and to modern ears questionable, charge of allegiance to a foreign prince has not been the deepest source of skepticism about Christians' political loyalty. When Rousseau makes his jab at Catholicism, he is only noting a particularly egregious example of what he regards as a more general problem: that traditional Christian belief has always given people "two homelands." For Christianity directs our hearts and minds toward the promised land beyond the grave and commands us to strive for the rewards of eternal rather than temporal life. In Rousseau's words, "The Christian's homeland is not of this world." Nor is it only the enemies of the faith, like Rousseau, who attest to this difficulty. St. Augustine famously declared that Christians' primary loyalty is not to the cities of this life, but rather to the City of God, which, in his words, "calls out citizens from all nations and so collects a society of aliens"—aliens, that is, in our own sense of those who are not citizens and whose loyalties are therefore likely to be divided. Similarly, in one of his favorite metaphors, Augustine describes the City of God as passing through this world "like a pilgrim in a foreign land" and our life on earth as "the time of our pilgrimage, in exile from the Lord."

Fostering love of country, then, has always been recognized as a problem, and it has posed special difficulties, in different ways, for liberals and Christians. Since most of those reading this are likely to be Christian liberals of one stripe or another, this is a matter worthy of further consideration. Must the state simply accept that we cannot, in the end, be counted upon? Assuming that we cannot really pull off a version of Plato's noble lie, even if we wanted to, should citizens simply conclude that the best thing to do in a pinch is cut and run? Or is there some way that we—even we Christian citizens of a liberal state—can justify loving our country in the way it seems to require?

Why Do People Love Their Country?

There are, I think, two basic reasons why people are likely to love their country. The distinction between the two is suggested nicely by the words of a love song from the old Rodgers and Hammerstein musical *Cinderella*. The song asks the question, "Do I love you because you're beautiful, or are you beautiful because I love you?" Anyone who has been in love will immediately recognize the difficulty of answering that question. We might love someone because of certain good qualities that person possesses—beauty, for example, or virtue. We might, however, attribute those good qualities to our beloved precisely because we are already, for some other reason, in love. Anyone who has ever wondered about a smitten friend, "What could she possibly see in him?," will recognize the problem. For the truth is that love, though not, as some claim, blind, does see with eyes of its own.

> *Those who consider their country worthy of their love only if it is good are doomed to perpetual disappointment.*

So also with love of country. We might think our country just, or noble, or a shining city upon a hill, and love it on account of its good qualities. On the other hand, we might be more inclined to attribute justice or nobility to our country, precisely because we already love it for some other reason. But why would we love it, if not for its good qualities?

The answer, I think, is not hard to find. Most of us, I suspect, love our country for the very simple reason that it happens to be our home. The love of home is surely among the most common and universal human feelings. So many memories are bound up with one's native land; so many friends and neighbors inhabit its familiar places; well-known and fondly remembered sights and sounds, even the very smells, can arouse deep inner longings and stir our hearts.

> **❝** *Parents love their children even when they are not beautiful; and they love them even when they are not good.* **❞**

Recently I had occasion for the first time in several years to drive through the part of northeastern Ohio, near Cleveland, where I grew up. As we drove through the city and I caught glimpses of old familiar sights, I could feel the excitement growing within me, and it was with great pleasure that I pointed out to my four-year-old son the Terminal Tower, the best-known landmark in Cleveland's skyline. In a certain sense—as my wife insisted on pointing out—this was mildly ludicrous, because the small town where I grew up is actually about thirty miles west of Cleveland, and I probably wasn't in the city itself more than a few times a year, usually for an Indians game. But that only serves to illustrate my point: even though Cleveland itself had not been my home, it was close enough and bound up with enough memories, like going to ballgames with my father, that just driving through the city and seeing its skyline could warm my heart. The familiar sights of home can do that. And this emotion goes far toward explaining why most people love their native land. Most of us, most of the time, probably love our country less because it is good than simply because it is ours.

Should Loyalty Be Based on Goodness?

Is either of these two possible motives for loving country—that it is good, or that it is ours—preferable, or even defensible? Given this choice, we are likely, I think, to be drawn toward the first option: loving our country because it is good. The second—loving it merely because it happens to be ours—seems almost irrational, less a reason than an emotion, little more, indeed, than a prejudice. A common prejudice, no doubt, but a prejudice hardly becomes more justifiable simply by being widely shared. The first motivation, by contrast, appears to be not only a reason, but a good reason, perhaps even the best one imaginable. Presumably our country is worthy of our love precisely to the extent that it is good—to the extent that it is just, free, humane, generous. And how could we continue to love a country that we knew lacked these qualifies? Surely we would not recommend loyalty to a state we considered unjust. Christians, especially, may be drawn to this point of view. We are commanded to love one another and to serve our neighbors, and we have been granted some insight into what a truly just city would be like. Should we not love the actual earthly countries in which we live when they strive to pattern themselves on the model of that Heavenly City and reject them when they do not?

But loyalty based upon a country's goodness or justice is potentially a very dangerous thing. Indeed. Christians are particularly well-positioned to see this, for they understand that our earthly polities are, in truth, never fully just. As Augustine pointed out long ago, "true justice is found only in that commonwealth whose founder and ruler is Christ"—the City of God, and not in any of our earthly cities. Those who consider their country worthy of their love only if it is good are doomed to perpetual disappointment.

> *It does not seem troubling for people to love . . . their children and parents, their husband or wife, their friends. Why should their country be any different?*

Disappointment, however, is not the worst effect of such dashed hopes. The frustration of those who, dissatisfied with the shortcomings of political life, wish to make it measure up to some ideal standard of justice, religious or secular, can be a lethal phenomenon. Edmund Burke saw the results of this frustration already in the French Revolution, but we have numerous more recent examples of those who, unwilling to love a country stained by imperfection, chose, regardless of the cost, to substitute some preferred vision of their own for the country they actually inhabited. Their names provide a roll call of the twentieth century's greatest atrocities: Hitler, Stalin, Mao, Pol Pot. That century was littered with the corpses of those who paid the price for these tyrants' unwillingness to love their country unless it became, in their own eyes, beautiful. As Burke put it, by hating vices too much, they came to love men too little.

Loving What One Has Been Given

Is not the second alternative, however—moving my country merely because it is my own—equally bad? This appears to be nothing more than a form of narrow parochialism, an attitude nicely captured in a play by John Galsworthy entitled *Loyalties*. The tragedy of this play is generated by problems of social class and ethnic prejudice, and Galsworthy emphasizes the destructiveness of such loyalty to one's own. In a striking passage at the center of the drama, one of the characters notes that such loyalties are indistinguishable from mere prejudice and can only create unresolvable conflicts: "Prejudices, Adela—or are they loyalties—I don't know—criss-cross—we all cut each other's throats from the best of motives." If loyalty to one's own country is only a prejudice of this sort, it is likely to produce a "my country, right or wrong" attitude. And such an attitude seems most conducive to a kind of self-serving nationalism that places one's own country above all others. It may be true that the twentieth century witnessed much ideological fanaticism, but surely it also taught us the dangers of proud, self-interested jingoism and nationalist fervor. Perhaps frustrated love-of-the-good produces destructive revolution, but chauvinistic love-of-our-own easily leads to ethnic conflict and outright war among peoples. That is little more than a choice between devils. If these are our options, it might be best to give up on love of country altogether and see whether we can muddle through without it.

From a purely secular perspective, it may well be difficult to prevent the simple love of one's own from descending into dangerous nationalism. From a Christian perspective, however, there is actually a very good reason for this love of one's own. We can begin to understand what this reason might be by thinking for a moment not about love of country, but rather about a different kind of love, that of parents for their children. Children and countries share an important characteristic: we do not normally choose them. Rather, they are simply presented to us, and we take what we get. Parents love their children even when they are not beautiful; and they love them even when they are not good. Indeed, a parent who made his love conditional upon a child's maintaining some particular standard of virtuous behavior would be rightly regarded as something of a monster. Naturally, parents hope their children will become good, and they normally spend considerable time and effort trying to bring about this desirable result. But the child's goodness is not the reason for his parents' love; they do not love him because he is good. Parents love their children, rather, simply because they are their children.

> *Christians . . . are precisely the kind of patriots that a decent polity should want to have.*

This, I think, makes perfectly good sense from a Christian perspective. Christians are called to love as God loves us, which ultimately means to love every human being as a unique individual, in the fullest sense of that overused term. For most people, the family is the arena in which we are most profoundly challenged to attain this goal, because it is in the family that we most regularly, directly, and intensely encounter other people in the full uniqueness of their personality, with all of their foibles and idiosyncracies, all the hidden nooks and crannies of the soul that are never fully revealed but of which family members, for better and for worse, catch privileged glimpses. This little world of rich human interaction is the first and fundamental, though not the only, context in which we are called to learn what it really means to love another human being, however different he may be from us. And in this task the exquisite arbitrariness of the gift of children is a tremendous advantage. For it means that we cannot go easy on ourselves by picking those whom we are predisposed to like, or with whom we share important interests, or who are likely to become rich and famous; we must simply take whoever comes. The Christian, however, will not find this unreasonable, for the particular children whom we receive are, of course, not really arbitrary at all. We did not select them, it is true, but they were nevertheless chosen, and chosen for a purpose, by one whose wisdom is greater than ours; and we trust that He knows what He is doing. And so parents love their children, not because they are good, but because they are the ones whom God has given.

Appreciating God's Gifts

With this model of parental love before us, we are in a better position to understand the significance of loving that which is our own. That significance arises from what we might call the meaningfulness of our context in a particular place and time. I have suggested that we accept our unchosen children as a gift whereby God seeks to teach us the meaning of love by calling us to the task of loving these particular individuals. But those children are only one part of the broader context into which God has placed us, and that context—in which we learn the concrete meaning of love by learning to love concrete, particular persons—is, like the children, largely independent of our choosing. We can affect parts of it, of course, but in large measure it is simply given. We do not choose the town where we are born or raised; we choose neither our children nor our parents; many people in the world, of course, do not even choose their spouse, who is chosen for them; indeed, we do not even choose our friends exactly, since, though we select them to an extent, we do so from among those who merely happen to be around us. And, of course, we do not choose our country. The broad context of our lives is largely not of our choosing. Yet it does not seem troubling for people to love their hometown, their children and parents, their husband or wife, their friends. Why should their country be any different?

This may seem like a peculiar conclusion. Why should we feel any love for the arbitrary results of fate? In a certain sense it is true that what I have been calling our context is simply a matter of chance. From a Christian perspective, however, that is only a partial truth. For from that perspective, our context— the place in which we find ourselves, the people by whom we are surrounded—is charged with moral meaning, because God has placed us there. It is our context, the one that He has given us, and if we have eyes to see and ears to hear, then we are called to appreciate the goodness of His gifts. Like parents called to love the children they have not chosen, we are all called to love those around us, for whom God has made us at least partially responsible. He has given us, so to speak, a charge, and if we refuse our stations, it suggests that we think Him mistaken to have placed us here. In its own way, an unwillingness to occupy those stations reflects that desire to be the Author of the play, and not a mere character in it, that under other circumstances we would not hesitate to call the sin of pride. Accepting with love and gratitude our context, the place and people whom God has given us, is one way of recognizing that we are creatures who, unlike our Creator, must live in a particular place at a particular time.

> *[Christians] love their country, not because it is good, but because it is given.*

But doesn't this noble rhetoric still conceal a danger, one suggested, in fact, by the Rodgers and Hammerstein verse alluded to earlier? "Do I love you because you're beautiful, or are you beautiful because I love you?" If we love our country, not because of any goodness or beauty it may possess, but simply because it is our own, do we not become prone, like the lover in the song, to attribute to it a beauty or a goodness it does not possess? Are we not likely to make of it a false god? This is indeed a danger, one against which we must remain continually vigilant. But it is much more of a danger, I think, for the secular nationalist than for one operating from the Christian perspective I have sought to describe here. For nothing in my argument requires making any special claim of superiority on our own behalf; quite the contrary, it relies heavily upon the assumption that no country can claim to be truly just or good. To love our country in the way I have described we need not imagine that it is ultimately better or more virtuous than any other. The differences we observe in other countries need give rise to no hostility, nor need we seek to assert ourselves at others' expense. . . .

We can readily recognize the value of other, different ways of life. For just as we cherish the country God has given us, others may cherish their own country as the one God has given them. National chauvinism will not grow well in such soil.

Love of the Good

Though I have sought to defend love of country on the basis of loving one's own, love of the good surely plays some role in a healthy patriotism as well. This is perhaps best expressed in negative terms: although we do not love our country because it is good, we might have to cease loving it were it to become particularly wicked. Or (perhaps better) if there were still a sense in which we continued to love it even then, we could not, at any rate, act on that love as we might under other circumstances. Love of the good thus sets limits of a sort on love of our own. Similarly, even if we love our country because it is ours, and not for the sake of a goodness it does not possess, we can still strive to make it better, just as parents strive to make their children good without ceasing to love them when they misbehave.

Loving our country because it is good and loving it simply because it is ours are thus both important; ultimately, neither perspective can stand entirely alone. They are not, however, equally in need of defenders. For if our country were ever to become truly good, it would be obvious enough that we should love it; and there is, in our contemporary world—and especially in the academy—no shortage of people hectoring us and insisting, in harsh and accusing tones, that we should certainly not love it until it becomes much better than it is today. We are much less likely to be reminded that we may—and, if my argument is persuasive, should—love it, warts and all, simply because it is ours. Christians, however, should not be afraid to say this. After all, neither my wife, nor my children, nor my friends have achieved perfection any more than my country has, yet no one would criticize me for loving them. They are God's gifts to me and are to be cherished for that reason. And if their Giver can love me with all my blemishes and imperfections, then surely I can love His gifts in the same spirit. One's country should be counted among those gifts.

In a sense, then, Rousseau missed the point when he criticized Christianity for giving us "two legislative orders, two rulers, two homelands." It is true that Christians inhabit this world "like a pilgrim in a foreign land," longing for that city where we will find our perfect rest. But our loyalties are not thereby divided; they are multiplied. The one who learns to love the great Giver of all life will not suddenly forget how to love His gifts; nor will he who worships the God who is Love find his own capacity for love diminished. In Bonhoeffer's wonderful image from the passage at the head of this essay, "Where the ground bass is firm and clear, there is nothing to stop the counterpoint from being developed to the utmost of its limits." Christians, then, are precisely the kind of patriots that a decent polity should want to have. They know that their country has its faults. But they do not imagine that it can earn their love only by becoming faultless. They love their country, not because it is good, but because it is given.

Organizations to Contact

The editors have compiled the following list of organizations concerned with the issues debated in this book. The descriptions are derived from materials provided by the organizations. All have publications or information available for interested readers. The list was compiled on the date of publication of the present volume; the information provided here may change. Be aware that many organizations take several weeks or longer to respond to inquiries, so allow as much time as possible.

American Civil Liberties Union (ACLU)
125 Broad St., Eighteenth Fl., New York, NY 10004
(212) 549-2585
Web site: www.aclu.org

The ACLU is a national organization that works to defend Americans' civil rights guaranteed in the U.S. Constitution. The ACLU publishes the quarterly newspaper *ACLU in Action* as well as the briefing papers "A History of Fighting Censorship," and "Preserving Artists' Right of Free Expression." Its Web site has a searchable archive of articles on religious liberty, students' rights, free speech, and other civil liberties issues.

American Enterprise Institute (AEI)
1150 Seventeenth St. NW, Washington, DC 20036
(202) 862-5800 • fax: (202) 862-7177
e-mail: info@aei.org • Web site: www.aei.org

The American Enterprise Institute for Public Policy Research is a scholarly research institute that is dedicated to preserving limited government, private enterprise, traditional values, and a strong national defense. It publishes a bimonthly magazine, *American Enterprise*, and *On the Issues*, a monthly compilation of articles and editorials. Reports and papers such as *America After 9/11: Public Opinion on the War on Terrorism and the War with Iraq* and "Polls on Patriotism" are available on its Web site.

Brookings Institution
1775 Massachusetts Ave. NW, Washington, DC 20036
(202) 797-6000 • fax: (202) 797-6004
Web site: www.brookings.org

The institution, founded in 1927, is an independent think tank that conducts research and education in economics, business, government, and the social sciences. Its goal is to improve the performance of American institutions and the quality of public policy by using social science to analyze emerging issues. Its publications include the quarterly *Brookings Review*, periodic *Policy Briefs*, and books such as *America Unbound* and *Cultivating Democracy*.

Cato Institute
1000 Massachusetts Ave. NW, Washington, DC 20001-5403
(202) 842-0200 • fax: (202) 842-3490
e-mail: cato@cato.org • Web site: www.cato.org

The Cato Institute is a libertarian public policy research foundation dedicated to limiting government and protecting individual liberties. It offers numerous publications on public policy issues, including the triennial *Cato Journal*, the bimonthly newsletter *Cato Policy Report*, and the quarterly magazine *Regulation.*

Center for the Study of Popular Culture
PO Box 67398, Los Angeles, CA 90067
(310) 843-3699 • fax: (310) 843-3692
e-mail: info@cspc.org • Web site: www.cspc.org

This educational center was started by commentators David Horowitz and Peter Collier, whose intellectual development evolved from support for the New Left in the 1960s to the forefront of today's conservatism. The center offers legal assistance and addresses many topics, including political correctness, multiculturalism, and discrimination. In 1993, the center launched a national network of lawyers called the Individual Rights Foundation to respond to the threat to First Amendment rights by college administrators and government officials. The center publishes the online *FrontPage* magazine.

Eagle Forum
PO Box 618, Alton, IL 62002
(618) 462-5415 • fax: (618) 462-8909
e-mail: eagle@eagleforum.org • Web site: www.eagleforum.org

Eagle Forum is a Christian group that promotes morality and traditional family values as revealed through a conservative interpretation of the Bible. It opposes many facets of public education and liberal government. The forum publishes the monthly *Phyllis Schlafly Report* and a periodic newsletter.

Fairness and Accuracy in Reporting (FAIR)
112 W. Twenty-seventh St., New York, NY 10001
(212) 633-6700 • fax: (212) 727-7668
e-mail: fair@fair.org • Web site: www.fair.org

FAIR is a national media watchdog group that investigates conservative bias in news coverage. Its members advocate greater diversity in the press and believe that structural reform is needed to break up the dominant media conglomerates and establish alternative, independent sources of information. *Extra!* is FAIR's bimonthly magazine of media criticism.

Heritage Foundation
214 Massachusetts Ave. NE, Washington, DC 20002-4999
(202) 546-4400 • fax: (202) 546-8328
e-mail: info@heritage.org • Web site: www.heritage.org

The foundation is a conservative public policy research institute that advocates limited government, free-market economics, individual freedom, and traditional values. Its publications include the monthly *Policy Review*, the *Backgrounder* series of occasional papers, and the *Heritage Lecture* series.

Institute for Policy Studies (IPS)
773 Fifteenth St. NW, Suite 1020, Washington, DC 20005
(202) 234-9382 • fax: (202) 387-7915
Web site: www.ips-dc.org

The Institute for Policy Studies is a progressive think tank that works to develop societies built around the values of justice, diversity, and nonviolence. It publishes reports, papers, and books such as *The Pre-Emptive Empire: A Guide to Bush's Kingdom* and *Liberalism: The Genius of American Ideals*.

Media Research Center
325 S. Patrick St., Alexandria, VA 22314
(703) 683-9733 • (800) 672-1423 • fax: (703) 683-9736
e-mail: mrc@mediaresearch.org • Web site: www.mediaresearch.org

The center is a watchdog group that monitors liberal influence in the media. Its programs include a news division that analyzes liberal bias in mainstream news coverage. The center's publications include *Media Reality Check*, a weekly report on news stories that have been distorted or ignored, and *Flash Report*, a monthly newsletter. The Web site also offers *CyberAlert*, a daily e-mail report on national media coverage.

National Coalition Against Censorship
275 Seventh Ave., New York, NY 10001
(212) 807-6222 • fax: (212) 807-6245
e-mail: ncac@ncac.org • Web site: www.ncac.org

The coalition represents more than forty national organizations that strive to end suppression of free speech and the press. It publishes a quarterly newsletter, *Censorship News*. Other publications include the brochure "25 Years: Defending Freedom of Thought, Inquiry and Expression," and the booklet (produced in collaboration with the National Educational Association) *Public Education, Democracy, Free Speech: The Ideas That Define and Unite Us*.

People for the American Way Foundation
2000 M St. NW, Suite 400, Washington, DC 20036
(202) 467-4999 • (800) 326-7329
e-mail: pfaw@pfaw.org • Web site: www.pfaw.org

People for the American Way Foundation is a nonprofit, nonpartisan organization that opposes the political agenda of the religious right. Through public education, lobbying, and legal advocacy, the foundation defends the right to dissent and opposes proposals to ban flag desecration. The foundation's Web site includes Right Wing Watch, an online library of information about right-wing organizations, and the Progressive Network, a database with links to progressive organizations across the country.

War Resisters League (WRL)
339 Lafayette St., New York, NY 10012
(212) 228-0450 • fax: (212) 228-6193
e-mail: wrl@warresisters.org • Web site: www.warresisters.org

The WRL, founded in 1923, believes that all war is a crime against humanity and advocates nonviolent methods to create a just and democratic society. It publishes the magazine *The Nonviolent Activist*. Articles from that magazine, as well as other commentary about America's war against terrorism, are available on its Web site.

Bibliography

Books

William J. Bennett — *Why We Fight: Moral Clarity and the War on Terrorism.* New York: Doubleday, 2002.

Walter Berns — *Making Patriots.* Chicago: University of Chicago Press, 2001.

Anne Coulter — *Treason: Liberal Treachery from the Cold War to the War on Terrorism.* New York: Crown Forum, 2003.

William Crotty, ed. — *The Politics of Terror: The U.S. Response to 9/11.* Boston: Northeastern University Press, 2004.

Henry A. Giroux — *The Abandoned Generation: Democracy Beyond the Culture of Fear.* New York: Palgrave Macmillan, 2003.

Mark Green, ed. — *What We Stand For: A Program for Progressive Patriotism.* New York: Newmarket Press, 2004.

Jesse Kornbluth and Jessica Papin, eds. — *Because We Are Americans: What We Discovered on September 11, 2001.* New York: Warner Books, 2001.

Dennis J. Kucinich — *A Prayer for America.* New York: Thunder's Mouth Press, 2003.

Julianne Malveaux and Reginna A. Green, eds. — *The Paradox of Loyalty: An African American Response to the War on Terrorism.* Chicago: Third World Press, 2002.

Michael Moore — *Dude, Where's My Country?* New York: Warner Books, 2003.

Cecilia Elizabeth O'Leary — *To Die For: The Paradox of American Patriotism.* Princeton, NJ: Princeton University Press, 1999.

William Rivers Pitt — *Our Flag, Too: The Paradox of Patriotism.* New York: Context Books, 2003.

Norman Podhoretz — *My Love Affair with America: The Cautionary Tale of a Cheerful Conservative.* New York: Free Press, 2000.

Howard Zinn — *Declarations of Independence.* New York: Perennial, 2003.

Periodicals

Paul Begala — "Sunshine Patriots: Stupidity Doesn't Stop at the Water's Edge," *American Prospect*, November 5, 2001.

William J. Bennett   "A Nation Worth Defending," *USA Today Magazine*, November 2002.

Jolene Chu and   "The Flag and Freedom," *Social Education*, October
Donna P. Couper   2003.

Ruth Conniff   "Patriot Games," *Progressive*, January 2002.

Craig Cox   "Grand Old Flag," *Utne Reader*, November/
                         December 2002.

Economist   "Home of the Brave," November 8, 2003.

Jonah Goldberg   "Fourth Is a Time to Celebrate, Educate—but Not
                         Debate," *Los Angeles Times*, July 4, 2004.

Stephen Goode   "Patriot Politics: Political Disagreement Is as Old as
                         America, but Critics Still Are Debating When Prin-
                         cipled Dissent Ends and Seditious Opposition Be-
                         gins," *Insight on the News*, June 24, 2003.

Loyd Grossman   "Why We Love the Flag and the Frontier: Ameri-
                         can Patriotism May Seem Mawkish, but It Has
                         Deep and Abiding Roots," *New Statesman*, Decem-
                         ber 17, 2001.

Victor Davis Hanson   "Loyalty, How Quaint," *National Review*, Novem-
                         ber 24, 2003.

Lee Harris   "The Intellectual Origins of America-Bashing," *Pol-
                         icy Review*, December 2002/January 2003.

Orrin G. Hatch and   "Give Old Glory a Vote," *American Legion*,
Tim Hutchinson   November 2002.

Rich Heffern   "Flying the Colors," *National Catholic Reporter*, Oc-
                         tober 12, 2001.

Robert Jensen   "Saying Goodbye to Patriotism," *Witness*, March
                         2002.

Michael Kazin   "A Patriotic Left," *Dissent*, Fall 2002.

Stuart Lutz   "Seasons of the Flag: After Years of Ups and
                         Downs, Old Glory Has Just Made Its Greatest
                         Comeback," *American Heritage*, February/March
                         2002.

Martha C. Nussbaum   "Can Patriotism Be Compassionate?" *Nation*, De-
                         cember 17, 2001.

Richard D. Parker   "Homeland: An Essay on Patriotism," *Harvard Jour-
                         nal of Law and Public Policy*, Spring 2002.

Tony Platt and   "Patriot Acts," *Social Justice*, Spring 2003.
Cecilia O'Leary

Lawrence W. Reed   "The True Meaning of Patriotism," *Ideas on Liberty*,
                         June 2003.

David Warren Saxe   "Patriotism Versus Multiculturalism in Times of
                         War," *Social Education*, March 2003.

Sam Smith   "How to Be a Patriot," *Yes! A Journal of Positive Futures*, Spring 2002.

Robert Stevens   "A Thoughtful Patriotism," *Social Education*, January/February 2002.

Howard Zinn   "Dying for the Government," *Progressive*, June 2003.

Index